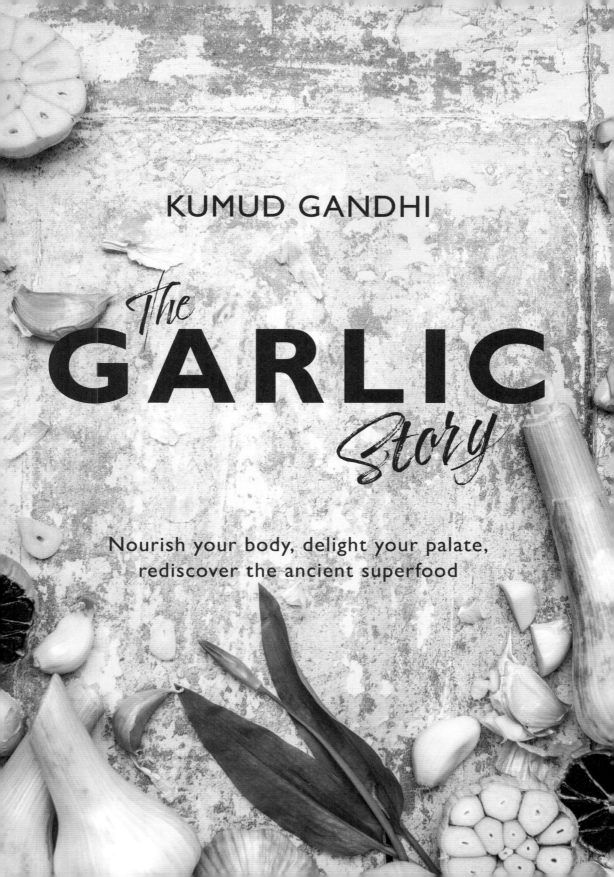

KUMUD GANDHI

*The*
# GARLIC
*Story*

Nourish your body, delight your palate,
rediscover the ancient superfood

©2023 Kumud Gandhi &
Meze Publishing Ltd. All rights reserved
First edition printed in 2023 in the UK
ISBN: 978-1-915538-10-9
Written by: Kumud Gandhi
Edited by: Katie Fisher & Phil Turner
Photography by: Paul Gregory
(www.PaulGregoryPhotography.co.uk)
Additional photography: Ian Bannister
Designed by: Paul Cocker
Sales & PR: Emma Toogood & Lizzy Capps
Contributors: Lis Ellis, Sam Borland,
Rhianna Emberson, Vicky Frost,
Kate McCann, Emily Retford
Printed by: Bell & Bain Ltd, UK

Published by Meze Publishing Limited
Unit 1b, 2 Kelham Square
Kelham Riverside
Sheffield S3 8SD
Web: www.mezepublishing.co.uk
Telephone: 0114 275 7709
Email: info@mezepublishing.co.uk

# CONTENTS

## GARLIC IN EUROPEAN CUISINE

# GARLIC: A LIFELONG CULINARY LOVE AFFAIR

*"One rule in life,"* he murmured to himself. *"If you can smell garlic, everything is all right."* – J.G. Ballard, High-Rise

Garlic is divine. Few ingredients can produce flavour in so many distinct ways when cooked correctly. Nothing is more beautiful than delicately roasted garlic, simply popped into the oven whole with all the cloves still on the bulb; it gets mellower and sweeter, ready to be squeezed out of the skins once soft and unctuous. When I smell garlic cooking in butter, it evokes so many emotions, transporting me immediately to lazy holidays in sunnier climes or simply making me feel that everything is alright with the world. Over the years, as I have learned more, cooked more and experimented with garlic more, it has become my superhero, an ingredient that lifts my spirits and brightens my day. It's the one ingredient I would never be without, and I seldom feel guilty that I may have garlic breath… there are worse things to worry about!

As well as its many flavours and dimensions, garlic is a mighty powerhouse of nutritional value that supports our biology and bodily functionality in so many ways and comes with an incredibly rich history throughout the millennia. So, it tastes great and it's good for us: it's not hard to see why I have such a glowing adoration for this humble vegetable!

Misuse of garlic is a crime in my book, not only in the way you cook it but also the way in which it's prepared; it should be treated with the greatest respect. There are many ways to prepare this wonderful vegetable. If you are slicing, be sure to use a sharp knife, or crush it with the flat of the blade, but do not use a garlic press (as Anthony Bourdain believed, it is too brutal an instrument for something that deserves such tenderness). It is the delicate use of garlic that makes the most profound difference to a recipe. Using 'lazy garlic' from a jar is of course forbidden and anyone admitting to that in my cooking classes would be ejected immediately; if you can't be bothered to peel it then surely you simply don't deserve this beautiful gift from nature! When I slice fresh garlic – to rub onto a piece of bread or insert tiny slivers into incisions I have made in a joint of meat – I hold my hands to my face after rinsing them and joyfully inhale the garlic perfume lingering on my skin. I could easily wash it away but why would I? It's the aroma of anticipation and the promise of a wonderful meal in the offing.

So, garlic haters steer clear now! The recipes in this book celebrate everything that's amazing about healthy, aromatic and flavourful garlic. I know for some, garlic is the devil incarnate and it receives a bad rap with its strong, unmistakable flavour. The key to cooking garlic is to tame that punch and the recipes in this book will show you how to enjoy garlic the way it should be enjoyed: with delight, reverence, and anticipation. I want to demonstrate that, when prepared correctly, garlic-centric dishes are nothing but delicious. Armed with the right information, you will then be able to experiment with adding a little (or a lot) more garlic to your home cooking, in everything from classic garlic bruschetta to my wild garlic pesto.

Why would anyone write a book solely focused on garlic, you may be asking? Surely, it's the most commonplace of vegetables, loved and loathed in equal measure but nothing to get excited about. But here's the thing, this humble allium – tossed without much thought into our sofritos and stir fries – not only adds depth of flavour but also boasts a host of significant health benefits alongside a rich and interesting history.

Garlic has been on the culinary radar for more than 5,000 years and has been used in many guises including medicines, aphrodisiacs, currency, and even magic potions. Preserved garlic was discovered in the tomb of Tutankhamen and in ancient Greek temples. The commonly held belief that garlic was able to ward off disease and ailments was deeply embedded in ancient civilisations and, even more interestingly, cultures that developed in isolation all came to the same conclusions about the efficacy of garlic. It's the vegetable that crops up in every single cuisine, bar none: exciting ways to cook with garlic are a feature of every culture.

The essence of this book is to make garlic the main guest at the table: to show you ways to use garlic as more than just a flavour enhancer or another base ingredient. Garlic is so much more than the sum of its parts and can be enjoyed in many ways: as a vegetable, as seasoning, in a pesto or butter, or my particular favourite, confit. Unlike a conventional meat confit which is a meal in itself, my garlic confit is a saviour that has come to the rescue of many a bland dish. If you have garlic and oil, you have confit… and if you have confit, you can have many wonderful things, from soups, salads and spreads to inner peace!

I view garlic as a great gift bestowed on us by Mother Nature, to be respected and utilised with care and imagination. Unless you are allergic to it or have an aversion to its flavour, garlic will quietly underpin most dishes in your weekly repertoire. Herein lies its appeal: most of us already cook with it and know that it adds wonderful flavour and aroma; it's a familiar ingredient that we feel comfortable with. At the same time, many of us secretly long for some inspiration to get us off the recipe treadmill. Garlic's versatility can offer us this inspiration, because whether you look to Europe, Asia, or the Middle East, garlic is the common denominator for a world of diverse flavours and cooking techniques.

Those who delve more deeply into this book will be surprised to learn about the fascinating history of garlic and, more importantly, its varied proven health benefits such as lowering cholesterol and blood pressure: it is antibacterial, antiviral, antimicrobial, and the most primitive form of antibiotic. Most importantly, this is a cookery book, packed full of straightforward but delicious recipes, featuring dishes from all over the globe, and conveniently categorised into sections. My aim for this book to inspire you, the reader and cook, to explore a range of flavour profiles and learn to use garlic in all its dimensions. Alongside my recipes, I hope that the pages relating to garlic's medicinal properties and historical context will help to create a shift in your perception of garlic, encouraging you to fully embrace this hugely underestimated gem of an ingredient.

# WHAT'S SO GOOD ABOUT GARLIC?

There are so many reasons to include garlic in your diet. In culinary terms, the pungent taste of garlic becomes mellow and sweet when cooked and adds an umami base level of flavour to stews, curries, stir fries, and pretty much everything else, as well as having an enticing aroma. Used raw, such as crushed into a dipping sauce, the cloves will enhance and accentuate the other ingredients. Try roasting a whole head of garlic for deliciously sweet, caramelised cloves to spread on freshly griddled sourdough. Garlic is a BIG ingredient, but often people don't know how to use it. If they did, they would love it as much as I do!

Put simply, cooking with garlic just makes everything taste so much better; sometimes garlic and salt are the only ingredients I will use to season a dish. The plant itself is so versatile too as you can use every part of it; chop up the stems and treat them as you would chives, while the flowers have an intense garlicky flavour and are great in salads as well as making a beautiful garnish for savoury dishes. There's very little you can't make with garlic: dips, dressings, marinades, butters, sauces, oils, mayonnaise, pickles, soups, stews, vegetable dishes, tea (yes, tea!), ferments, and even ice cream (check out The Garlic Farm on the Isle of Wight) are all enhanced by this wonderful ingredient.

For all its apparent robustness, garlic can be a delicate flower and it is therefore important to know how to prepare it correctly. First, put down that garlic press: its brutal action crushes the clove harshly, affecting the flavour and leaving a good deal of the clove behind, plus it's a pain to wash! Better by far to employ a trusty chef's knife. Remove the papery skin and finely chop the garlic, continuously running your knife through the garlic until the desired consistency is achieved. To mince garlic, sprinkle chopped garlic with a generous pinch of coarse salt and then use the flat of your knife to press and smear the garlic against the chopping board. The more you damage the cell walls of the garlic, the stronger the flavour will be, so an intact clove is the mildest of all, followed by sliced garlic, with minced garlic being the strongest, although the addition of salt mitigates the harshness.

To achieve the maximum health benefits from your chopped or sliced garlic, leave it to sit on your board for 10 minutes before applying heat. During this time healthy sulphide compounds will form, particularly allicin. This not only boosts flavour and aroma, but allicin is crammed full of health benefits too. These benefits are denatured by heat, but by delaying the cooking process for 10 minutes the maximum amount of allicin is created and remains intact during cooking.

When cooking with garlic, ensure you add the wetter ingredients first (onions, for example). These will release water as they cook, preventing the garlic from burning. Burnt garlic will taint the whole dish and there's nothing for it but to start over again, so cook it gently and with care. To further maximise the nutritional value, you could wait to add the garlic until the last few minutes of cooking.

Many people are wary of raw garlic, fearing that it will be pungent and overpowering. Think of fabulous spicy salsas, gorgeous gazpachos and punchy salsa verde though: they all contain raw garlic and they taste great because the power and heat of the garlic is beautifully balanced and harnessed by the other ingredients.

Once you get the garlic bug it's fun to branch out and experiment a little. How about trying black garlic? Black garlic is simply fresh raw garlic that metamorphoses over time to become sweet, tangy, deeply umami and, surprisingly, not particularly garlicky. It pairs beautifully with mushrooms, makes a mean vinaigrette and an absolutely delicious hummus. Introduce it to lamb and pasta dishes or throw a few cloves into a tray of roasties: like the raw form, it's astonishingly versatile. Another type of garlic you won't want to miss is wild garlic. It's seasonal of course (March to June) but foraging for wild garlic (or ransoms, as they are otherwise known) is always time well spent. The plants love damp soil in woodland and their aroma is unmistakeable, so follow your nose and look for their bright white flowers and long green leaves (see page 26 for more information). Once you've brought your haul of wild garlic leaves home, flick through the recipes in this book for inspiration on how to cook them, or if you're feeling more adventurous, try making wild garlic soup, bake a piece of fish wrapped in the leaves, or wilt them in olive oil and toss into scrambled eggs or an omelette. Like the rest of the garlic family, it's refreshingly versatile.

Just what is so good about garlic? In a word: everything!

# TYPES OF GARLIC

Garlic is a versatile and flavourful ingredient used in many culinary preparations and recipes. I enjoy cooking with garlic in all its forms. Traditionally, garlic was used in the classic bulb and fresh leaf form throughout the centuries. As its popularity has grown, many more forms of garlic have become available, including fresh green garlic strands, wild garlic leaves, black garlic, and dried varieties.

Broadly speaking, there are three basic types of garlic bulbs. The hard neck variety is the hardiest of these, forming its cloves through a process of vernalisation whereby the garlic is exposed to cold temperatures by staying in the ground over winter. There are usually between four and twelve cloves in each bulb. One of the benefits of hard neck garlic is the way their skins slip off smoothly. However, the disadvantage is that hard neck garlic doesn't keep as long as other types, lasting only five to six months (which may only be relevant if you are considering growing them yourself). Within the hard neck variety there are eight different types of garlic: Asiatic, Creole, Purple Stripe, Glazed Purple Stripe, Marble Purple Stripe, Porcelain, Rocambole and Turban. Creole garlic is perhaps the rarest of all these. The 'neck' in the name refers to the stalk that grows upward from the garlic bulb; hard neck stalks stem from the centre of the bulb and turn rigid at maturity.

Soft neck garlic tends to be the most used variety. The fresh bulb is dried after harvesting to become the papery garlic bulb we know and love, with a longer shelf life of up to 12 months when stored correctly. This is because soft neck garlic is more densely wrapped in its skins which means there's less chance of moisture or disease getting in. Soft neck garlic has leaves rather than a central stalk that remain flexible at maturity and can be braided for storage (it's often sold this way in the Mediterranean). There are only two types of soft neck garlic, silverskins and artichokes, with a much more limited selection of cultivars to choose from.

Then there is elephant garlic, which is not a true garlic but rather a type of leek. It produces three to six enormous cloves in each bulb that look like garlic but have a much milder flavour, though this may turn sharp or occasionally bitter in cold climates. In very cold regions it may produce one single bulb like a pearl onion rather than dividing into cloves. Like hard neck garlic, elephant garlic forms flower stalks; the lower parts of the seed stalk can be used in stir fries and other dishes.

## WILD GARLIC – RAMSON

Ramsons are wild garlic plants that you may notice during a springtime walk in the woods. They grow well in the shade and occasionally in sun, producing white flowers as well as edible leaves and bulbs. The leaves are best enjoyed before the flowers bloom in late spring and have a delicate garlic flavour that can be enjoyed raw, particularly in salads and pesto. When cooked, ramsons lose that flavour, developing more of an oniony taste instead. I like to use the flowers to decorate my salads or other dishes, and they are delicious to just eat! In my family, ramsons have always been used to stimulate digestion, as an antimicrobial agent, as a detoxing food, and to treat respiratory illnesses such as colds and flu. During their short season, ramsons are very much enjoyed in culinary delights as well as for their medicinal benefits. The bulbs, when harvested, can be used like any other type of garlic, but I would strongly urge you to only take the bulbs if you have grown them in your own garden, in the interests of preservation and encouraging the wild reseeding process. Taking whole plants from the wild is a definite no-no in the environmental rule book. Once established in your own garden, they will keep coming back year after year as long as you leave some bulbs in the ground.

## GREEN GARLIC

Green garlic is an immature garlic plant that looks like a cross between a leek and a spring onion. Instead of eating the bulb, the whole plant is harvested, the bulb discarded, and the green stalk is eaten; this has a delicious garlicky flavour that can be used in both cooking and salads. From March to October, I am rarely without green garlic and use it for almost anything. The taste is somewhere between a chive and a salad onion, slightly veering towards a mild garlic flavour. It can be sprinkled liberally over most foods; I happily make flavoured butter with it to melt over omelettes, scrambled eggs, pizza, rice, or noodles. However, I think my greatest use of green garlic is with potatoes; this makes a blissful match, and you'll find a variety of recipes for this combination throughout this book.

## BLACK GARLIC

I have recently come to enjoy black garlic for its surprising subtlety. Black garlic is essentially aged garlic, made with fresh raw garlic that changes over time due to low heat and high humidity, in a process called the Maillard reaction. During this process, the cloves turn black and their texture and flavour changes. Black garlic is softer, smoother, chewier, and has a sweet molasses-like taste, as well as a little tang not unlike balsamic vinegar or even tamarind. It's used to enhance the flavour of many dishes, and while black garlic may seem like a fad or a recent phenomenon, it's been around for centuries. Though the origins are unclear, early documentation records black garlic in Asia, though it is used in a great deal of European recipes too. Black garlic can be sliced, chopped, smashed, or puréed for stirring into soups, sauces, stews, pastas, and sautéed vegetables. You can buy bulbs or pots of black garlic which can be kept at room temperature for up to three weeks or refrigerated for up to six months. Black garlic paste is also available and equally as delicious; it has a wonderful mellow flavour that adds unctuousness. Unlike raw garlic, it doesn't have the pungency to overwhelm a dish, so you may need to add more than you think if you're using other strong flavours.

## GARLIC SCAPES

Scapes can be harvested from hard neck garlic in the spring. The scape is the flowering stalk that grows in the middle of hard neck garlic bulbs. If left to grow, the green stem will curl and form a white bulb, but it is usually removed so that the plant will not produce more seeds and will instead grow a bigger bulb. If you are planting garlic and wish to use the scapes in cooking, it's better to harvest the scapes when they first come up before the stem gets woody and more difficult to snap off. Scapes are often available in farmers' markets so be sure to pick some up if you see them; they are delicious and simple to cook, tender and crisp sautéed in butter or olive oil, delicious in pesto.

## DRIED GRANULATED GARLIC

Granulated garlic is simply dried garlic that has been coarsely ground to a sand-like consistency. It's made by drying fresh garlic cloves in an oven, then grinding the cloves into granules. It is often used as a seasoning in dry rubs, spice blends and even breadcrumb coatings such as for fishcakes or vegetable burgers, because of how well it distributes the garlic flavour without adding moisture. It's also a useful backup ingredient if there were ever a rare catastrophe and you ran out of garlic. I sometimes sprinkle it over a slice of pizza to add some umami flavour... though I wouldn't ever mention that to my Italian friends! You can usually find granulated garlic in the seasoning aisle of your local supermarket.

## GARLIC POWDER

Garlic powder is made of dehydrated garlic cloves that have been dried and finely ground to a flour-like consistency. The fine consistency allows the garlic to disintegrate and be incorporated into a recipe quickly. Garlic powder tends to have the most concentrated and pungent flavour, though it can be made subtler by diluting with water. For example, I add garlic powder to the pasta water while boiling in order to season the pasta as it cooks. You can also add garlic powder to meats for a burst of flavour without impacting the moisture levels. The difference between garlic powder and granulated garlic is the consistency, so you should decide which to use based on what you are trying cook and how you are going to be cooking it. Garlic granules are less likely to clump than powder which may affect the consistency of a rub or spice blend; you may wish to sieve the powder to avoid clumps.

# HOW TO GROW GARLIC

Luckily, garlic is an easy plant to grow and – as with anything – the most important thing is to have fun with it. My connection to food is important to me, so I like watching things grow and using ingredients fresh from the garden in my cooking. I feel a greater sense of investment which fills me with a terrific amount of pride and joy. I hope my guidance on how to grow garlic will give you some encouragement to have a go too.

Autumn is the best time to plant before there is any chance of the ground freezing in the winter months. Garlic likes full or partial sun. Most garlic growers recommend full sun, though my garlic only gets sun in the morning and does very well. In really hot climates garlic may do better with afternoon shade to help shield garlic from the full heat of the day and prevent the leaves from browning.

## PREPARE THE SOIL BEFORE PLANTING

For the larger bulbs, prep your garlic bed well. Garlic loves a rich fertile loam soil or a silty loam soil and needs the soil to be well drained to thrive. Soggy bottoms are a complete no-no as the garlic will simply rot. The soil should also be rich in organic matter, and if it isn't then you may need to improve it with some manure, humus or compost and till it thoroughly. In addition, garlic is a heavy feeder which means it likes lots of nutrients such as nitrogen, phosphorus and potassium. Adding organic matter will give you the biggest and best tasting garlic.

## PREPARE THE GARLIC BULBS

Carefully separate each garlic bulb into individual cloves. Each clove will grow a new bulb of garlic. Handle carefully so the cloves don't get damaged in any way as cuts and bruises could provide entry points for rot during the winter.

## PLANT THE GARLIC CLOVES

Plant the garlic clove 10-15cm deep. In areas with colder winters, you should plant the garlic at least 12-15cm deep and 10-15cm apart. I tend to space mine 12cm apart in rows, with the rows 18cm apart. You can make individual holes using a blunt handle (such as the end of a rake or shovel) or a bulb planter. Alternatively, you could dig a trench 10-15cm deep, then lay in the garlic cloves and cover. The most important thing is to plant the garlic with the pointed end at the top.

## WEED AS NECESSARY

In late winter or early spring you will see your garlic sprouts emerging. Keep the plot well weeded; it is hard for garlic to compete with weeds and can reduce the harvest significantly if left unchecked.

## WHEN TO FERTILISE

Fertilising the garlic bed will ensure you get a really tasty and nutritious crop, so add nitrogen at least once during the growing season before the garlic comes up through the ground – otherwise you'll end up with more leaves than garlic.

## WATERING

Hard neck garlic bulbs are ideally suited for dry climates; most garlic will do fine on regular winter rainfall during the growing season. However, you may want to water in the spring or early summer if it is really dry. Don't keep the soil constantly moist or you risk garlic rot.

## HARVEST THE GARLIC

Ideally the garlic should start drying out in early summer. The bottom leaves will start to dry out and turn brown. Garlic is ready to harvest when only the top 4-5 green leaves are left. Be careful not to leave it in the soil too long or the bulb quality will start to deteriorate. Dig or gently pull your garlic (if the soil is soft it will be easier to pull up the bulbs). Do not remove the stems yet.

## STORAGE

Hard neck garlic cannot be braided for storage as the stems are hard. Instead, place the garlic bulbs in a cool dry area with good air movement for 4-6 weeks. Some people hang garlic, we dry it on racks. The garlic bulbs can be eaten immediately raw and will have a more mellow flavour, while the ones stored for longer will have a stronger flavour. Once the stems are dry you can clip off the bulb and store it in a dry airy place.

## HOW LONG TO KEEP GARLIC

The length of time that garlic will keep for depends on your storage conditions. For the longest storage time, place garlic in a cool, dry area at 10°c such as an unheated room. Do not store garlic in plastic or airtight containers as this will cause mould and rot. Garlic will sprout if exposed to prolonged temperatures below 6-7°c.

## ELEPHANT GARLIC

Follow the directions above but increase the spacing between cloves to 25cm. Plant from September.

## WILD GARLIC

Plant the cloves 2-5cm deep, 25cm apart. Keep well-watered during the first year and don't pick any plants. Wild garlic seed heads should also produce viable seed and assist in the spread of your wild garlic area.

## ROCAMBOLES

Hard neck types produce beautiful floral spikes. These can be snapped off almost as soon as they appear to encourage the plant's resources back down towards the bulb. Also known as scapes, these can be sautéed and enjoyed like a garlicky green bean, or even made into a delicious pesto.

## GREEN GARLIC

Growing green garlic couldn't be easier and if I have garlic bulbs that are beginning to grow green shoots, I instantly use them to grow green garlic.

**Planting:** Simply separate the bulbs into individual cloves, keeping the papery skin on the clove. Sit the cloves on a wet tissue paper or sponge on a window ledge until they sprout roots on the base, which should happen within 2-3 days. Don't use any cloves that have become soft. Fill a tray or pot with a general peat-free multi-purpose compost and water it. Unlike regular garlic that likes space, for green garlic the garlic cloves can be planted up to 5cm deep with the pointed end upwards and 4cm apart. Keep the soil moist until the cloves germinate because if they dry out they may not germinate, but if the soil is waterlogged they will rot. In just 4 weeks you'll have fabulous green garlic strands to harvest that resemble chives, only thicker and stronger. If you're having a particularly harsh winter, you could start them in a warm place indoors to enjoy them early.

**Feeding and Watering:** Keep the soil evenly moist throughout the growing season but make sure it is not waterlogged at any time. Feed the plants by mulching or use a general organic fertiliser.

**Harvesting:** Harvest the green garlic either by cutting off stalks as required or pulling up the whole plant when it has reached the required size. Although green garlic can be pulled up at any stage, the longer you wait to harvest, the more pronounced the bulb will be. Don't wait until the leaves start to die back as you will want to use the whole plant.

# FORAGING FOR WILD GARLIC

Wild garlic, also known as ramsons, is a perennial plant that can be found in the UK from late March to June when it grows in abundance in damp shady deciduous woods, creating a beautiful carpet of lush green leaves with white star-like flowers. The leaves are long, pointed oval shapes with untoothed edges. They grow from the base of the plant and have an unmistakeable garlicky scent.

Foraging for wild garlic leaves is hugely enjoyable; that first foray into the woodland after a typical British winter is joyful, a sign that spring is finally here and there is much to look forward to. Then there is the anticipation that you'll find an early crop of fresh vibrant green leaves to make something delicious with, to please the palate like nothing else. For me, the first recipe I make with wild garlic has to be a jar of deep emerald-green pesto, a jewel to adorn my pasta or sourdough.

Wild garlic is a delicious and versatile ingredient that is easily recognised by its distinctive garlic-like aroma. Early in the season, the fragrance may not be so pungent but if you think the plant looks right, just rub the leaf between your fingers and you'll soon notice the familiar scent. When identifying wild garlic, look out for its broad, glossy, slightly curved leaves. The small, star-shaped, white flowers are also a good indicator, although they bloom later in the season so if you're an early bird you may only find the leaves. When picking wild garlic, use scissors or a sharp knife to cut the leaves just above the ground. Never harvest the bulbs; leave them intact in the ground so that the plant can continue to grow the following year.

If you're interested in foraging for wild garlic, the best place to start is in ancient woodlands, along riverbanks, and in damp clearings. Wild garlic can also be found in hedgerows and along the edges of fields. When you're out foraging, be sure to always follow the countryside code so that you forage without causing any damage to the natural environment, and only pick what you need. That way, you'll have another reason to go back and benefit from the freshness of the leaves every time!

# WHAT DOES
# WILD GARLIC LOOK LIKE?

Flowers: small and white, with six petals on a thin stalk. Around 25 flowers form each rounded flower cluster which is held high on a single, leafless stalk.

Fruit/seeds: wild garlic reproduces through bulbs, bulbils and very occasionally seeds. The seeds are 2-3mm long, black and flattish on one side. They are dispersed when the parts of the plant above ground die down.

Not to be confused with lily-of-the-valley when not in flower, though the leaves of wild garlic grow from the plant base whereas lily-of-the-valley has two or three leaves on its stem. When in flower, lily-of-the-valley is easily distinguishable from wild garlic as it has bell-shaped, white flowers. Lily-of-the-valley is poisonous so be sure to fully identify wild garlic before foraging.

Wild garlic leaves have a lighter flavour profile than that of garlic bulbs so if you enjoy the more subtle form of garlic, you're in for a treat. The leaves and flowers are both edible and can be eaten raw in salad, blanched and used in place of spinach, or made into amazing soups and pesto. I have included recipes for these throughout the following chapters in this book. I hope you enjoy foraging for and cooking with wild garlic as much as I do.

# A GARLICKY HISTORY LESSON

## *"The king of herbs"*

The word garlic derives from Old English and its literal translation means a leek with a spear. Disparagingly known as 'Italian perfume' or 'the stinking rose', garlic is one of the very few ingredients to be represented within every global cuisine and one of the oldest documented vegetable crops. Loved and loathed in equal measure, garlic has been revered as an offering fit for the gods and reviled as suitable only to be fed to swine. This most profitable of all vegetables is shrouded in mystique and for more than 5,000 years has been used not only as an ingredient but as medicine, an aphrodisiac, currency, and even as a magic potion. Exciting ways to cook with garlic pop up in every culture and while fabulous recipes lie at the heart of this book, we shouldn't ignore the rich history and amazing properties of this fascinating foodstuff.

The very first accounts of garlic date back 5,000 years ago to the Old World cultures of Egypt and India. Historical evidence shows that the Babylonians were using it 4,500 years ago and there is also evidence to suggest that garlic was grown in China up to 4,000 years ago. Preserved garlic was discovered in the tomb of Tutankhamun and was regularly consumed by Ancient Greek and Roman soldiers and by the African peasantry. Today, garlic grows wild only in Central Asia but historically it is believed to have grown throughout India, Egypt and Ukraine. It is believed that the Sumerians introduced garlic to China and from here it made its way to Japan and Korea. Garlic is even mentioned in the Bible; when the Jews followed Moses out of Egypt is it recorded that they missed "the fish, the cucumbers, and the melons, and the leeks, and the onions and the garlic" (Numbers 11:5).

Considered to be a 'performance enhancing agent', garlic was distributed to labourers in many cultures and even administered to Greek athletes to propel them to Olympian heights. Early Greek military leaders fed their armies with garlic before major battles. The Romans also valued garlic as an aid to strength and endurance and it was routinely fed to both soldiers and sailors as well as forming part of a ship's manifest when it set sail. In Ancient Egypt garlic was used for mummification and even accompanied the dead on their final journey into the world beyond. The Chinese valued garlic as an effective element in food preservation, while in Korean folklore 20 cloves of garlic and a bundle of mugwort were sufficient to transform a bear into a woman, Ungnyeo.

"Do not eat garlic or onions; for their smell will reveal that you are a peasant." – Cervantes, Don Quixote.

It was the Crusaders who brought garlic to Europe, and the Spanish, French and Portuguese who introduced it to the Americas. During the medieval period garlic really rose to prominence in Europe, although it was considered to be the food of the peasant classes. In ancient India the higher classes avoided garlic because of its pungent odour and association with the common herd. In the court of King Alfonso de Castile, knights reeking of garlic would be expelled and exiled for a week. Similarly in England, garlic was considered to be beneath dignity for the young ladies and gentlemen of high society and America followed suit by not embracing garlic until as late as the 1940s. The arrival of immigrants from Poland, Germany and Italy helped to create a demand for garlic in America where it is now a kitchen staple.

The higher echelons of British society, however, were not immune to the therapeutic values of garlic, even as it was considered the diet of the working classes. Thanks to the medieval monks who gained and promulgated knowledge of the therapeutic use of plants, garlic was recommended for constipation, toothache, dropsy, animal bites, and the plague. Doctors carried cloves of garlic with them at all times to protect themselves from the unpleasant odours of disease.

In the western world the use of garlic rapidly expanded during the Renaissance, beginning in Italy before moving to France and ultimately through the rest of Europe. King Henry IV of France was instrumental in enhancing the popularity of garlic by rubbing his royal grandson's lips with a clove of garlic to protect him from the "evil eye" and bestow on him the power to lead the nation. King Henry was himself baptised in garlic water to protect him from evil spirits and disease. It is widely believed that the cultivation of garlic commenced in England before the 16th century, where wild garlic was actively grown in church courtyards. In England during the Victorian era, garlic was embraced by the great and good when all things French were considered to be the height of taste and sophistication. From there on, the use of garlic became firmly embedded in British cuisine.

Throughout history garlic has been carried by migrants both for consumption and cultivation. It is a hardy plant that is resistant to many diseases and pests and grows well in a variety of soils and conditions. This has allowed garlic to become widespread as well as increasing its popularity. Globally garlic has been both hailed and shunned. Certain religious orders firmly believe that garlic has the power to inflame the passions and its consumption is forbidden (more on this from page 40). Chinese doctors prescribed garlic for men with 'intimacy problems', while grooms placed cloves of garlic in their buttonholes to ensure a successful wedding night and a happy honeymoon. Unfaithful Egyptian husbands might chew garlic on their way home from their mistresses to hide the scent of another woman. Myths, truths and half-truths serve to shroud garlic in mystique. Nestled deep within the cloves of this commonplace ingredient lies a rich history alongside a wealth of myth and folklore.

# GARLIC IN MYTH AND FOLKLORE

We all know that garlic keeps those pesky vampires away but according to legend, garlic was used to ward off all sorts of nasties. Demons and werewolves too could be held in abeyance with the judicious use of a clove or two. The name 'allium' is in fact linked to an ancient Celtic word, all, which meant 'monster slayer', confirming that this vegetable was used to ward off evil spirits, vampires and witches. Considered a precious amulet, garlic took on a very important role as a good luck charm, so much so that it was given to those in difficulty.

Medieval folk believed that garlic protected against the evil eye and therefore hung it over their doors. Its mythical powers extended to protecting maidens and pregnant ladies; Ancient Greeks placed garlic on piles of stones at crossroads as a supper for Hecate, a goddess of the wilderness and childbirth, or to ward off evil spirits and cause them to lose their way thus protecting people from demons. As the centuries passed, this ancient custom became commonplace in most European homes.

Despite its reputation for warding off evil and use as a medicinal herb, garlic was considered too coarse and common for the refined palates of the upper and religious classes in many cultures throughout the world. Only the rough lower classes could eat garlic, as it would upset the delicate constitutions of the rich and powerful. Egyptian priests worshipped garlic but actively avoided cooking and eating the fragrant cloves.

In Asian culture the Koreans of old ate pickled garlic before passing through a mountain path, believing that tigers disliked it and therefore ensuring a safe journey. In Palestinian tradition, if the bridegroom wears a clove of garlic in his buttonhole, he is assured a successful wedding night. Among practitioners of Auryvedic medicine, garlic is held in high regard as an aphrodisiac and for its ability to increase the production of semen.

In England, garlic breath was also deemed entirely unsuitable for refined young ladies and the gentlemen who wished to court them. Many Americans adopted the English attitude and didn't embrace garlic until the 1940s. Until then it was considered an ethnic ingredient and known by slang terms such as 'Italian perfume'.

At the root of all this mythology, there is undoubtedly an irrefutable truth that garlic has health properties due to its unique composition. Despite somewhat humble and controversial origins, garlic is very much revered in the modern day for both its medicinal properties and its excellent flavour profile. I'm inclined to say that with better oral hygiene and a greater understanding of its chemical properties, we can also overcome the issue of 'garlic breath' much more easily! Happily, garlic consumption has increased dramatically throughout the world and is enjoyed in all its forms.

# GARLIC V. RELIGION

If you thought garlic was just an innocent, run-of-the-mill vegetable, think again. Simply by its very existence, garlic has been the cause of much controversy and soul searching in many of the world's great religions.

Throughout history, garlic has been both celebrated and condemned by the belief that it can inflame the passions of the soul. Certain sects of the Hindu tradition preclude garlic from their diet for this very reason, based on a traditional tenet that alliums, the genus that includes garlic and onions, adversely stimulate emotional and sexual excitement. Garlic is known as 'rajogini' which means a substance that makes a person lose their grip over their instincts and temperament.

Followers of Krishna and Swaminarayan regard garlic and onions in food as tamasic, as it disturbs the body's balance and can 'lower modes of nature which inhibit spiritual advancement to reach their ultimate goal of nirvana.' Tamasic foods are considered to overly stimulate the central nervous system and cause the body to emit odours which can linger for several days, which is considered disrespectful in the presence of the Lord or his saints. Furthermore, there is a belief that this stimulus may lead to unwanted feelings and sensations, and eventually cause them to break their vows of celibacy and calm nature.

For Brahmins, garlic is prohibited by scripture and considered impure, as it is believed to grow in places of impurity. It is essential to Brahmins that they maintain purity as they worship gods who are pure in nature. Garlic and onions are also forbidden to yogis "because they root the consciousness more firmly in the body" according to Dr Robert E. Svoboda, a leading authority on Ayurveda. For some, garlic is not just guilty of inflaming the passions and creating unpleasant odours but is also responsible for inducing intestinal gas (that's flatulence to you and me). For this reason, Buddhist monks avoid garlic as they believe that the internal disruption it causes hinders meditation.

In Taoism it is believed that garlic adversely stimulates emotional and sexual excitement. Some Buddhists also avoid consuming garlic, believing that it increases sexual desire when eaten cooked and anger when eaten raw. In Tibet, garlic was considered to inflame the passions and was forbidden to monks, widows, and adolescents. The Jain religion also eschews garlic, as it does all root and underground vegetables. This owes less to the stimulating nature of garlic and more to preventing injury to small insects and microorganisms, as well as preventing the entire plant from being uprooted and killed. Conversely the Talmud, the book of Judaism, prescribes a meal with garlic every Friday!

Religion's aversion to garlic does not rest solely on its effects as a stimulant; in many cases it's garlic's odiferous nature that is the problem. Ancient Greeks barred would-be worshippers from entering the temple if they failed a 'garlic breath' test. In Islam, Mohammed's writings equate garlic with Satan; he says that as the devil was cast out of the Garden of Eden, garlic sprang up where his left foot touched the earth, while onion emerged from his right footprint. Subsequently, Hadith instructed that "whoever eats garlic or onions should not come near our mosque" because both onions and garlic create bad breath. As mosques are to be kept clean and pure, unsullied by offensive odours, garlic lovers are required to pray at home.

Yet the Ancient Egyptians worshipped garlic as if it were a god and used it as local currency. Clay garlic bulbs were placed in Egyptian tombs with the dearly departed; archaeologists are unsure whether these were intended as funds for the afterlife or as idols to appease the gods. In addition, garlic was used to pay and feed workers and slaves on the great pyramids. The bulb was so popular with those who toiled on the pyramids that garlic shortages caused work stoppages. A garlic crop failure, due to the Nile flooding, caused one of the only two recorded Egyptian slave revolts.

It's hard to believe that today there are over 2.5 million acres of garlic cultivation… that's a lot of garlic for something that has had such a divisive journey through history! Who would have thought that such a tiny vegetable could create such controversy?

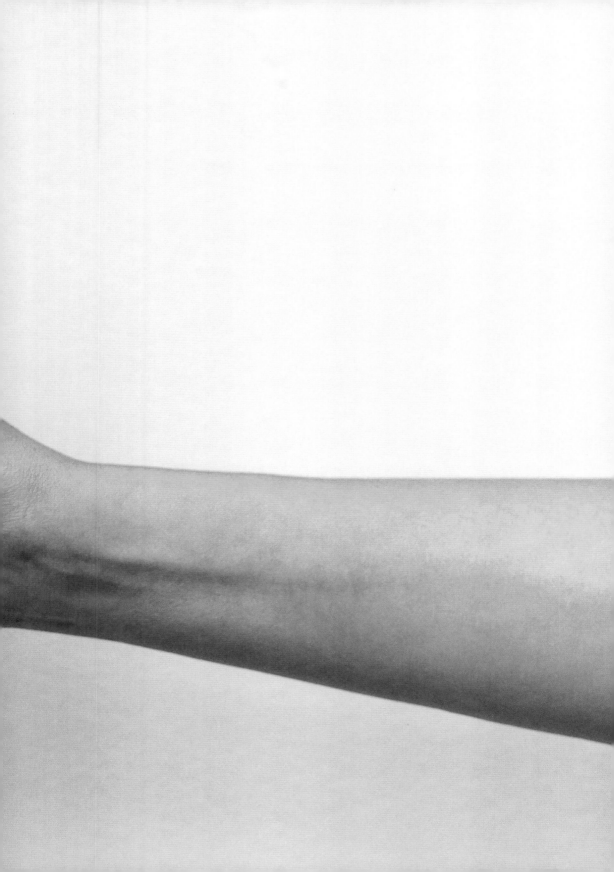

# THE HEALTH BENEFITS OF GARLIC

*An ancient medicine – a modern day cure-all.*

## THE SLAYER OF MONSTERS

Happily, there are numerous health benefits that stem effortlessly from consuming garlic and for you doubters, there is much evidence to attest to this. The humble bulb has been revered for thousands of years for its healing prowess and the benefits of garlic have origins in antiquity. Ancient medical texts from Egypt, Greece, Rome, China, and India each prescribed medical applications for garlic and are some of the earliest documented examples of plants used for medicinal purposes.

We know that garlic was in use at the beginning of recorded history and was found in Egyptian pyramids and Ancient Greek temples. Galen, the second century Greek physician, held garlic to be the 'rustic's theriac' – in other words, a cure-all. Another revered physician, Hippocrates, also prescribed garlic for a variety of conditions. There are many Biblical references to garlic and the Bhagavad Gita – the holy scripture of the Hindu faith – talks about the use of garlic as early as 5,000 years ago and further cites its use in Indian Ayurvedic medicine. The leading Indian ancient medical text, Charaka-Samhita, recommends garlic for the treatment of heart disease and arthritis over many centuries. In another ancient Indian medical textbook, the Bower Manuscript (c. 300 AD), garlic was used for fatigue, parasitic disease, digestive disorder and leprosy.

Fascinatingly, cultures that developed without contact with one another came to similar conclusions about the efficacy of garlic, and its use was prolific throughout all of Asia, Persia and Europe. Garlic was first brought to Britain in 1548 from the Mediterranean, then in 1564 a famed German professor and doctor recommended its use for a range of skin diseases. Louis Pasteur, the famous microbiologist, wrote in 1858 that garlic killed bacteria and he maintained it was effective even against some bacteria resistant to other treatments. The antiseptic properties of garlic were confirmed in its use against cholera in 1913, then typhoid fever and diphtheria in 1918. The French phytotherapist Lekrek used garlic as a preventive remedy with success during the Great Influenza or 'Spanish flu' pandemic. During the First World War garlic was used to treat wounds and amoebic dysentery, then employed widely as an antibiotic throughout the Second World War. Although penicillin was already in use by this time, the Russian Red Army continued using garlic and it was apparently renamed there as Russian penicillin: a natural antibiotic.

## GARLIC IN MEDICINE TODAY

Modern science, including nutrition, is now beginning to confirm many ancient beliefs about garlic, defining ways of using it and exploring garlic's potential for disease prevention and treatment. Recent laboratory tests have shown that garlic has antibacterial, antiviral and antifungal properties, thereby confirming what was earlier considered to be simple folklore. Further research is ongoing as to the possible medical uses of garlic and its extracts, while its status as a 'traditional' remedy has been solidified, which is a significant development for those who have always believed in the efficacy of garlic as a highly potent medicinal plant.

Clinical trials for the use of garlic in treating hypertension, high cholesterol and high blood pressure have seen great results and had excellent peer reviews from the medical world. Furthermore, new research has seen significant benefits in the prevention of cardiovascular and neurodegenerative diseases, cancer, and hepatic diseases. Researchers found that red blood cells turn the sulphur in garlic into a hydrogen sulphide gas which expands the blood vessels, making it easier to regulate blood pressure. Several medical publications have highlighted other features of garlic, including its antibacterial, antioxidative, antihypertensive, and antithrombotic properties. Garlic's antioxidant properties have been linked to the reduction of brain disorders such as Alzheimer's disease, and that's just the tip of the iceberg.

Other possible properties of garlic are also being investigated, including whether it can increase oestrogen levels in women entering menopause, a time when bones are most at risk of developing osteoporosis. Some studies have also shown garlic to slow the effects of osteoarthritis. While the preliminary studies are promising, more research needs to be done to confirm this connection.

Research by The Arthritis Foundation in conjunction with Cambridge University has shown that garlic oil works as an anti-inflammatory. If you have sore and inflamed joints or muscles, rub them with garlic oil; it's recommended to help prevent cartilage damage from arthritis.

A recent study has shown that the antibacterial and antioxidant properties of garlic can also kill bacteria that lead to food poisoning, including Salmonella and E. coli. In our classes at The Cooking Academy, we talk a great deal about how the ingredients we use today had traditionally been used for exactly these purposes prior to the availability of modern methods of food preservation and the extended shelf-life of many products as a result.

Professor Tim Spector, a leading epidemiologist and regular contributor to BBC Radio 4's The Food Programme, recognises the importance of garlic for a healthy gut microbiome and recommends its regular inclusion in our diets as one of the 30 plants necessary for good gut health.

## POWERFUL SMELL EQUALS POWERFUL HEALTH BENEFITS

Garlic gets its pungent smell from an organic sulphur compound called allicin, which is also where the goodness lies. One of the best ways to reap the benefits of garlic is by eating it raw, since it provides the greatest or most concentrated benefit to your health in this form. According to a study published by The National Library of Medicine involving 41,000 women between the ages of 55 and 69, those who routinely ate garlic had a 35% lower risk of colon cancer. The study cited that the active ingredient in garlic acts on multiple pathways to reduce the risk of gastrointestinal tumours.

So, how much raw garlic should you consume? One or two cloves of garlic a day is the optimal amount to get the most benefit without any of the undesirable side effects like body odour or heartburn. To make raw garlic more palatable, I prefer to slice the cloves thinly and sandwich them between apple slices. The apple will help cover up the pungent flavour, and mixing the garlic with another food makes the whole experience a lot more tolerable in my opinion! Another one of my tricks is to make garlic toast, by mincing the raw garlic and then mixing it with some ghee or butter to spread on toast. If you're still wincing at the idea of raw garlic sandwiches, try grating it into your salad, salad dressing, soups, smoothies or juices. The benefits to your body will be worth it!

# HINTS AND TIPS

When buying garlic, choose firm, plump bulbs that still have their paper-like skin intact. There should be no signs of sprouting, soft spots, or other blemishes. Fresh garlic is readily available year-round.

**Store fresh garlic in a cool, dark, dry place at 18°c with moderate humidity that is well ventilated for four to six months. Storing in a paper bag or mesh tubing works well. Avoid storing garlic in the fridge, as it tends to become somewhat tasteless.**

If garlic has been chopped, minced, or prepared in any way, it should be refrigerated and will last for up to seven days. Be sure to store the garlic in an airtight container to prevent the odour from affecting other foods in the fridge.

**Garlic cloves can range in size from small to extra-large, so when a recipe calls for a specific size, it is important to be aware of what that is referencing. I have included a guide here of the size differences and some information to help you determine if you are using the right amount of garlic that is called for in the recipe.**

An extra-large clove of garlic will be approximately 3.5cm long with a diameter of 2.5cm at the widest point.
A large clove of garlic will be approximately 3cm long with a diameter of 2cm at the widest point.
A medium clove of garlic will be approximately 2.5cm long with a diameter of 1.5cm at the widest point.
A small clove of garlic will be approximately 2cm long with a diameter of 1-1.5cm at the widest point.

1 garlic bulb equals 1 head, which is equivalent to 8-12 cloves.
1 small garlic clove equals ½ tsp when minced or ⅛ tsp of garlic powder.
1 medium clove equals 1 tsp when minced or ¼ tsp of garlic powder.
1 large clove equals 1½ tsp when minced or ¼ + ⅛ tsp garlic powder.
1 extra-large clove equals 2 tsp when minced or ½ tsp garlic powder.

**Peeling Hacks: You can place the garlic cloves in the microwave for 15 seconds and the skins should peel off easily. However, don't let the cloves get too warm, particularly if you're not going to use them all at once. Alternatively, once you've separated the garlic cloves from the bulb, drizzle the garlic cloves lightly in a neutral oil, leave the oil to work into the garlic for a few minutes, then gently rub them between your fingers; the skins will quickly loosen and fall off.**

**Storage Hack:** Keep peeled and minced garlic fresh by placing it in a small jar and pouring in just enough olive oil to cover the garlic, then placing it in the fridge. It will keep its fresh flavour for up to seven days.

Flavour Hack: Add a hint of super subtle but aromatic garlic flavour to your salad by cutting a raw garlic clove in half and rubbing the inside of your salad bowl with the cut edge of the clove.

**If you have sprouting garlic, it's a cardinal sin to throw it out! Instead, plant the cloves fairly close together in a pot or in the garden, even on a window ledge if the weather outside doesn't permit. The new shoots that appear will have a mild garlic flavour and can be used just like regular chives.**

To remove the odour from your hands when working with garlic, wash hands thoroughly and then use something made of stainless steel to work over and around the areas affected. I have a stainless steel tablet, much like a bar of soap, but you could easily rub your hands on a stainless steel pan. Stainless steel contains the mineral nickel which acts as a neutraliser for the garlic odour.

**Freezing garlic is an excellent way of preserving it to lock in the freshness and I do this routinely with mine; it's a monthly kitchen preparation task that ensures I always have an endless supply of minced garlic on hand for its many uses in cooking. Frozen garlic will last for up to six months but I doubt you'll have any left for that long! Fresh garlic can be frozen in several forms:**

You can freeze whole, unpeeled heads and remove cloves as you need them.

**You can wrap chopped or crushed garlic tightly in plastic wrap and freeze, then grate or break off what you need when required.**

You can peel whole cloves of garlic and purée them in a blender or mini food processor, using a splash of flavourless oil and a good pinch of salt, then freeze flat in a resealable plastic bag.

**Freshly peeled garlic cloves can be covered with oil and stored in the freezer.**

# GARLIC IN EUROPEAN CUISINE

I don't think it would be misleading to say that garlic is strongly associated with most European cuisines, particularly France, Italy and Spain. It might thus surprise you to know that garlic has long been treated with suspicion in Italy, being associated with poverty since Roman times and used to mask lesser quality ingredients. Famously, former prime minister Silvio Berlusconi wouldn't permit anyone in his cabinet to consume garlic while they were around him. Garlic is certainly not a staple in northern Italian cuisine and is more commonly used in southern Italy. To many chefs, great ingredients require little more than a splash of good oil and a pinch of salt. This is not to say that garlic isn't present in Italian cuisine, but rather that it is used in a more delicate fashion, simmering cloves gently in oil to release their sweetness or simply infusing a dish with garlic before removing it.

The reverse could be said of French cuisine, as French chefs employ the use of garlic generously in soups, stews and sauces. However, they understand how to tame the beast by including plenty of parsley to help counteract the lingering odour of garlic. They understand the art of patience too, often roasting or frying the cloves, or using them in confit form, where the heat and fat transform the garlic flavour, allowing it to be subtly integrated into dishes.

In Spain, garlic has been used in cooking for centuries and is one of the most important ingredients in Spanish cuisine. Here they celebrate its pungency; whether it's rubbing a cut clove over a piece of bread or starring as the main ingredient in a garlicky aioli, there's no getting away from the garlic!

Lightly smoked garlic is now being commonly used in British and other European cuisines, paired with poultry and game and making its way into soups and stews. Elsewhere in Europe, garlic regularly crops up in dips like aioli, skordalia and tzatziki. Scandinavian cooks adore wild garlic which is abundant in the spring, and love to use it in omelettes or as an alternative to spinach.

Let's not forget Eastern Europe too which gave us that iconic garlicky delight, Chicken Kiev. In Romania garlic appears on every menu and in the Baltic states, garlic, herbs and very little else are used as seasoning for meat and potato dishes.

Like a child in a sweet shop, when writing this book, my initial instinct was to take a deep dive into all the European cuisines, ferreting out and developing garlic-centred recipes from every corner of the region. Common sense finally prevailed on realising that the European chapter would give the Encyclopaedia Britannica a run for its money in size. So, with regret, I've had to cherry pick and edit the selection to what you'll find in the following pages. Nevertheless, I'm happy with the results which range from a quintessentially English tart featuring wild garlic, fabulous French cream of garlic soup, and stunning black garlic and lemon pappardelle. Best of all, there's nothing complicated about any of the recipes but with no compromise on flavour.

There's no doubt that garlic is deeply embedded in European culinary culture, so why not let your tastebuds do the travelling as you effortlessly rustle up a few garlicky showstoppers.

# ROASTED TOMATO CROSTINI WITH CONFIT GARLIC

**PREPARATION TIME: 10 MINUTES | COOKING TIME: 25 MINUTES | SERVES 4**

This recipe takes its inspiration from the classic Spanish pan con tomate. In my version, the tomatoes are simply roasted in the oven with a little thyme, salt and pepper, then piled onto slices of toasted sourdough that have been generously smothered in a blanket of my garlic confit (see page 164) to be unceremoniously scoffed. This makes a fabulous light lunch or even a breakfast dish, with more flavour than you can shake a stick at.

## INGREDIENTS

400g cherry tomatoes, halved lengthways

1 tbsp garlic oil (ideally taken from the garlic confit jar)

1 few sprigs of thyme, leaves only

1 fat garlic clove, finely minced

Salt and pepper

1 large garlic clove, halved

8 slices of sourdough

8 confit garlic cloves

Sea salt

## METHOD

1. Preheat the oven to 160°c/140°c fan/gas mark 3. Put the cherry tomatoes in a bowl with the garlic oil (or just use regular olive oil). Add the thyme leaves, minced garlic, salt and pepper to taste, then mix well and transfer to a roasting tin. Roast in the oven for 20-25 minutes.

2. Toast the sourdough when the tomatoes are almost ready and then rub each slice with the cut sides of the garlic clove.

3. Remove the tomatoes from the oven and lightly smash with the back of a fork. Spread a confit garlic clove (or more if you prefer) on each slice of bread, then pile on the roasted tomatoes along with a little of the garlic-perfumed oil.

4. Sprinkle the crostini with sea salt to taste, then garnish with fresh parsley or chives (or green garlic, if in season). Dive in and enjoy these simple foods at their best!

# BLACK GARLIC, LEMON AND CRÈME FRAICHE PAPPARDELLE

**PREPARATION TIME: 10 MINUTES | COOKING TIME: 10 MINUTES | SERVES 4**

How can a dish that tastes this luxurious be so easy to make? The secret weapon is black garlic, now easily found in most supermarkets, which gives the dish a sweet, tangy flavour with undertones of balsamic vinegar. The silky sauce is emulsified as you would a carbonara.

## INGREDIENTS

400g dried pappardelle

2 tbsp butter

1 tbsp olive oil

3 garlic cloves, finely sliced

2 sprigs of thyme, leaves picked

300ml crème fraiche

4 tsp black garlic paste

1 tsp flaky sea salt

1 tsp ground black pepper

1 lemon, zested

150ml reserved pasta water

2 egg yolks

75g grated parmesan

Handful of fresh basil leaves

## METHOD

1. Cook the pasta in well-salted water for 2 minutes less than the instructions on the packet. When you drain the pasta, make sure to reserve some of the pasta water for the sauce.

2. While the pasta is cooking, prepare the sauce. Add the butter and oil to a frying pan and gently fry the sliced garlic and thyme together for a couple of minutes until lightly golden. Remove the garlic with a slotted spoon and reserve to sprinkle on at the end.

3. Now stir in the crème fraiche and black garlic paste, then add the salt, pepper and lemon zest. Stir well, then add the pasta and drizzle in a little of the reserved cooking water, stirring gently to emulsify the sauce.

4. Take the pan off the heat and add the egg yolks one at a time, stirring to fully incorporate them in the residual heat. Finish the dish with the grated parmesan, the fried garlic and fresh basil torn over the top.

# GARLIC AND PARSLEY CRUSTED SALMON

**PREPARATION TIME: 15 MINUTES | COOKING TIME: 45 MINUTES | SERVES 4**

The popularity of salmon has increased over the years, not least because of its many nutritional benefits. Salmon is a rich source of protein, vitamin B, omega-3 fatty acids, selenium, and potassium. It's also a robust, meaty fish that can stand up to strong flavours. So, here's a new salmon dish to add to your repertoire; the gorgeous garlicky breadcrumbs add oodles of flavour and texture.

## INGREDIENTS

**For the marinade**

4 garlic cloves, finely chopped

2 tbsp olive oil

1½ tbsp lemon juice

1 tbsp chopped fresh coriander

1 tbsp finely chopped parsley

1 tsp ground cumin

½ tsp black pepper

¼ tsp salt

4 x 150g salmon fillets, skin on

**For the garlic and parsley crust**

40g butter

2 garlic cloves, finely minced

100g breadcrumbs

Salt and pepper

3 tbsp finely chopped parsley

Chopped chives or green garlic when in season, to garnish

## METHOD

1. Mix all the marinade ingredients together in a bowl, then add the salmon fillets and turn until well coated. Set aside to soak up the flavours for 30 minutes at room temperature.

2. Preheat the oven to 180°c/160°c fan/gas mark 4 or use a hot grill. Transfer the marinated salmon to a baking tray lined with baking paper. Place in the oven and cook for 12 minutes.

3. Meanwhile, make the garlic and parsley crust. Gently melt the butter in a frying pan, add the minced garlic and cook for 30 seconds, ensuring it doesn't burn, then add the breadcrumbs.

4. Fry the breadcrumbs until golden brown and slightly crispy. Remove from the heat and season with salt and pepper, then add the parsley and mix thoroughly.

5. When the salmon is cooked, remove it from the oven and transfer to a serving dish. Sprinkle the garlic and parsley crumb over the fish, then finish with a sprinkling of chives or green garlic strands if you can get them.

6. I like to serve this with steamed broccoli, tossed with one of my garlic butters (see page 180) and topped with any leftover garlic crumb, making it instantly more flavourful and tempting to eat!

# PRAWNS AND POTATOES IN GARLIC AND PIMENTÓN SAUCE

**PREPARATION TIME: 15 MINUTES | COOKING TIME: 35 MINUTES | SERVES 4**

This recipe is a tried and trusted favourite in our Mediterranean cookery class at The Cooking Academy. A hugely flavoursome dish with very few ingredients, it's a winner for quick and easy midweek cooking, typical of rustic Spanish cookery where a few simple ingredients are transformed into something satisfying and delicious. Slices of pan con tomate would make a worthy accompaniment.

## INGREDIENTS

400g Charlotte potatoes, peeled and sliced 1cm thick

4 tbsp olive oil

5 garlic cloves, thinly sliced

½ tsp chilli flakes

½ tsp smoked paprika

2 tsp sweet paprika

350ml fish stock

½ tsp salt

¼ tsp black pepper

500g large raw prawns, deveined and butterflied

Finely chopped parsley leaves, to garnish

Drizzle of fresh lemon juice

## METHOD

1.  Put the potatoes in a pan of cold salted water and bring to the boil. Simmer for 8-10 minutes or until just tender when pierced with the tip of a knife.

2.  Put the oil, garlic and chilli flakes into a deep frying pan over a medium heat. Let the ingredients sizzle gently for 3 minutes or until the garlic is lightly browned.

3.  Add the smoked and sweet paprika, then let the mixture cook for 20 seconds. Keep an eye on the heat level to ensure it doesn't burn. Add the fish stock, salt and pepper, then bring to the boil.

4.  Now add the parboiled potatoes to the pan and simmer vigorously for 10 minutes until the potatoes are soft and the sauce has reduced. Add a little more fish stock if the sauce seems too dry.

5.  Add the prawns and simmer for 3 minutes or until cooked. Garnish with parsley leaves and a tiny drizzle of lemon juice, then serve with crusty bread or pan con tomate.

# GORGEOUSLY GARLICKY ROASTED CHICKEN THIGHS

**PREPARATION TIME: 10 MINUTES | COOKING TIME: 1 HOUR | SERVES 4**

There's nothing shy or retiring about this dish. The garlic is up close and personal in every delightful bite but is mellow and buttery because of the way it's cooked. Accompanied by green vegetables and rice for mopping up all those tempting juices, there's every reason to dive in and enjoy!

## INGREDIENTS

8 chicken thighs (skin on, bone in)

1 tsp salt

½ tsp freshly ground black pepper

2 bulbs of garlic, separated into whole cloves (about 20)

3 tbsp olive oil

1 tbsp butter

2 tsp herbes de Provence

1 tsp plain flour

100ml chicken stock

½ lemon, juiced

## METHOD

1.  Preheat the oven to 180°c/160°c fan/gas mark 4. Pat the chicken dry with kitchen paper, then season with the salt and pepper. Remove the papery outer skins from the garlic cloves.

2.  Add the oil and butter to a large ovenproof frying pan and cook the whole garlic cloves over a low heat, stirring occasionally. After 10 minutes they should be lightly golden. Remove the garlic from the pan and set aside.

3.  Increase the heat to medium and brown the chicken thighs skin side down until golden and crispy, which should take approximately 5 minutes. Turn the chicken over and sprinkle with the herbes de Provence. Add the garlic cloves back to the pan and transfer to the oven.

4.  Roast the chicken for about 35 minutes or until cooked through. Once the chicken is done, place the chicken thighs and garlic on a warm plate.

5.  Place the roasting pan over a medium-high heat, sprinkle in the flour and stir to incorporate. Deglaze the pan with the stock and lemon juice to make a sauce.

6.  Pour the sauce over the chicken on the plate and squeeze the garlic cloves out of their skins over the top. Serve with rice for mopping up the sauce and some green vegetables.

# GARLIC AND LEMON GRILLED COURGETTES ON TOASTED SOURDOUGH

**PREPARATION TIME: 10 MINUTES | COOKING TIME: 15 MINUTES | SERVES 2**

For those of us who grow our own vegetables, it's often a job knowing what to do with a glut of courgettes. There's only so many chutneys and courgette cakes you can make! Here's an idea for a lovely light lunch, where courgette is enhanced by its friends, garlic and lemon juice. If you want to vary this, you could spread the sourdough with some soft lemony goat's cheese. Don't skimp on the toppings as they add wonderful flavour and texture.

## INGREDIENTS

2 courgettes

4 tbsp olive oil

3 tsp finely minced garlic

1 lemon, zested and juiced

¾ tsp sea salt

½ tsp black pepper

**To serve**

Sliced sourdough

Extra virgin olive oil

Pumpkin seeds

Onion seeds

## METHOD

1. First, roast the pumpkin seeds for the topping. Preheat the oven to 200°c/180°c fan/gas mark 6. Place a handful of pumpkin seeds in a bowl and drizzle over a little olive oil, just to lightly coat them. Season with salt and pepper, spread out on a baking tray and then roast in the oven for 7-8 minutes or until lightly browned and slightly crispy. Set aside on a plate to cool.

2. Meanwhile, thinly slice the courgettes lengthways using a vegetable peeler or mandoline. Put the olive oil, minced garlic, lemon zest and juice, salt, and pepper in a bowl (reserve the squeezed lemon for later). Mix well before adding the courgette ribbons, ensuring they are fully coated in the marinade. Set aside to marinate for a few minutes.

3. Heat a griddle or large frying pan until hot. Remove the courgettes from the marinade and cook for 1-2 minutes on each side until browned all over. You may need to do this in batches as each side should be fully touching the pan. Add the lemon halves at the same time, placed cut-side down in the pan. This will release more juice and give a lovely, caramelised flavour.

4. Meanwhile, toast the sourdough and drizzle with olive oil. Top each slice with the griddled courgette ribbons and a generous helping of roasted pumpkin seeds, finishing with a sprinkling of onion seeds.

5. This is even more delicious served alongside a burrata, also drizzled with olive oil.

# GARLIC BUTTER GNOCCHI WITH PURPLE SPROUTING BROCCOLI

**PREPARATION TIME: 10 MINUTES | COOKING TIME: 35 MINUTES | SERVES 4**

This is a great midweek supper, ideal when all you want is a big bowl of comforting goodness. The combination of garlic and chilli is a marriage made in heaven which is only enhanced by the bright citrus tang of the lemon.

## INGREDIENTS

300g purple sprouting broccoli, trimmed

500g gnocchi

1 tbsp butter

1 tbsp olive oil

½ lemon

### For the sauce

3 garlic cloves, finely sliced

1 tbsp olive oil

1 banana shallot, finely chopped

1 red chilli, finely chopped

50g butter

1 lemon, juiced

½ tsp Dijon mustard

30g parmesan, finely grated, plus extra to serve

Salt and pepper, to taste

## METHOD

1. Blanch the broccoli in salted boiling water for 3-4 minutes. Remove the broccoli with a slotted spoon and plunge into a bowl of ice-cold water to retain the colour.

2. Drop the gnocchi into the broccoli cooking water to simmer over a low heat according to the packet instructions. Drain the gnocchi, saving a little of the cooking water for the sauce.

3. Heat the butter and oil in a large frying pan, add the gnocchi and fry gently until lightly golden to give them a little texture. Remove from the pan with a slotted spoon and set aside.

4. Make the sauce in the same frying pan, starting with the sliced garlic. Separate all the slices in the pan to ensure they cook evenly, and just as they begin to develop a light golden hue, remove them from the pan with a slotted spoon, leaving as much oil in the pan as possible.

5. Now add half the olive oil with the shallot and cook slowly until it begins to develop a little colour. Stir in the chilli and cook for 2 minutes.

6. Now add the butter, lemon juice, mustard, parmesan, and plenty of seasoning to the sauce and cook on a low heat until the cheese has melted and everything is combined.

7. Keep the sauce warm over a low heat while you reheat the broccoli; heat the remaining olive oil in a frying pan, add the broccoli and fry until it starts to crisp up at the edges.

8. Now add the gnocchi to the sauce and stir to combine, adding a little of the reserved cooking water if you need to loosen the sauce.

9. Serve the gnocchi in warm bowls topped with the broccoli, an extra squeeze of lemon juice and more grated parmesan.

# GARLIC ROASTED TOMATO AND CHILLI LINGUINE

**PREPARATION TIME: 15 MINUTES | COOKING TIME: 20 MINUTES | SERVES 4**

Pasta is my go-to when I'm in a hurry and this recipe is as speedy as it gets, packed with unctuousness and deep flavours thanks to not one or two but three different uses of garlic! Don't let the simplicity fool you; by cooking a few humble ingredients together, you can create a delicious sauce with ease. Italian cookery is all about simplicity and celebrating produce, as this dish demonstrates.

## INGREDIENTS

24 baby plum tomatoes, halved lengthways

2 garlic cloves, finely minced

1 sprig of thyme, leaves only

6 tbsp olive oil

400g linguine

3 garlic cloves, peeled and thinly sliced

2 banana shallots, finely chopped

2 tsp finely minced garlic

1 bullet chilli, finely chopped or ¼ tsp chilli flakes

6 sprigs of thyme, leaves only

1 tsp Dijon or English mustard

½ tsp Himalayan salt

½ tsp black pepper

2 tbsp grated parmesan, plus extra to serve

240ml wine or thick vegetable stock

100g rocket

Handful of finely chopped parsley leaves

Drizzle of extra virgin olive oil

**Cook's Tip:** Add prawns, mussels, clams, or fresh crab meat to this dish for extra protein.

## METHOD

1. Preheat the oven to 180°c/160°c fan/gas mark 4. Place the tomatoes into a large bowl with the finely minced garlic, thyme leaves and 2 tablespoons of olive oil. Season generously with salt and pepper, mix well and then transfer to a large baking tray, spreading the tomatoes out so they don't sweat while roasting. Place in the preheated oven for 25-30 minutes or until golden and beautifully roasted.

2. Place the linguine into a pan of salted boiling water. Cook for 2 minutes less than the instructions on the packet. Drain, reserving the pasta water, then rinse thoroughly in cold water. Set aside.

3. While the pasta is cooking, heat the remaining oil in another pan. Add the sliced garlic, sauté in the warm oil for about 1 minute until the garlic is just getting golden, then remove from the pan with a slotted spoon, leaving as much oil in the pan as possible.

4. Now stir the shallots into the garlic-infused oil and cook on a low heat with the lid on until they have softened. This should take about 5-6 minutes.

5. Add the minced garlic and chilli to the shallots and cook for 2-3 minutes. Stir in the roasted tomatoes, thyme leaves, mustard, salt, and pepper. Cook for a minute or two to allow the flavours to infuse before adding the parmesan and wine or stock to the pan. Stir and bring to a simmer, then cook with the lid on for 1 minute.

6. Add the linguine, rocket and chopped parsley to the sauce. Stir everything together and toss with the lid on. Add some of the reserved pasta water (start with a tablespoon or two) if you want a little more sauce and a looser consistency.

7. Pile the pasta onto plates, drizzle with extra virgin olive oil and finish with a sprinkling of extra grated parmesan and the fried garlic slices for more texture and delicious flavour.

# GREEN GARLIC POTATO SALAD

**PREPARATION TIME: 10 MINUTES | COOKING TIME: 15 MINUTES | SERVES 4 AS A SIDE DISH**

Green garlic is simply immature garlic, with a flavour somewhere between spring onions and mature garlic. It makes a delicious dressing, and this recipe takes me straight back to my childhood as my mother would regularly use green garlic in her recipes.

## INGREDIENTS

1kg baby potatoes

3 tbsp finely chopped parsley leaves (or dill if you prefer)

A handful of chive flowers, to garnish (optional)

**For the green garlic dressing**

20 fresh green garlic stalks, finely chopped (20g)

2 tsp finely minced garlic

3 tbsp mayonnaise

2 tbsp honey

1 tbsp cider vinegar

½ tsp black pepper or to taste

¼ tsp salt or to taste

## METHOD

1. Scrub the potatoes and cut them into quarters lengthways, ensuring they are all a similar size to allow even cooking. Boil the potatoes in salted water until firm but cooked through, about 15 minutes.

2. To make the green garlic dressing, simply combine all the ingredients. This will keep in the fridge for several days.

3. Now mix the dressing with the cooked potatoes, parsley or dill, and chives if using. Add the dressing a little at a time as you may not need all of it, but it's certainly worth making a little extra as it's delicious and you can use it with all sorts of other dishes.

4. Taste to check the seasoning, adding a little salt and pepper as required, then enjoy!

# CREAM OF GARLIC SOUP WITH GARLIC CROUTONS

**PREPARATION TIME: 1 HOUR 20 MINUTES | COOKING TIME: 1 HOUR 30 MINUTES | SERVES 4**

Garlic, garlic and more garlic: what could be more divine! My creamy garlic soup recipe calls for four bulbs of garlic – yes, that's right, bulbs not cloves! – but stay with me a few moments longer and judge me not. While raw garlic is a powerful ingredient that can feel like a sharp elbow to the tastebuds, in this recipe I'm using roasted garlic which is an entirely different ball game. Once roasted, fresh garlic cloves take on a sweet, mellow, almost nutty flavour. These are the bedrock of my soup, yielding nothing but flavoursome bowls of comfort.

## INGREDIENTS

4 bulbs of garlic

2½ tbsp olive oil

¼ baguette (preferably stale)

1 tsp minced garlic

¾ tsp salt, or to taste

¾ tsp black pepper, or to taste

2 banana shallots, finely diced

600ml vegetable stock (or chicken stock if you prefer)

100g parmesan, grated

250ml double cream

Finely chopped fresh parsley, to garnish

## METHOD

1.  Preheat the oven to 180°c/160°c fan/gas mark 4. Trim the tops off the garlic bulbs, just enough to expose all their cloves. Pour over half a tablespoon of olive oil and sprinkle with a little salt and pepper. Place each bulb cut side down on a small square of parchment paper foil. Fold the paper around the bulb to make a neat parcel and place on a baking tray. Roast for 45 minutes, then leave to cool completely before pressing the garlic out of its skins.

2.  Meanwhile, make the garlic croutons. Cut the baguette into 0.5cm squares, then mix with 1 tablespoon of the olive oil, the minced garlic, and a quarter teaspoon each of salt and pepper. Spread the croutons out on a baking tray and once the roasted garlic is done, turn the oven up to 200°c/180°c fan/gas mark 6. Bake the croutons for 7-8 minutes until crispy and golden. When ready, set aside to cool.

3.  Heat the remaining oil in a frying pan and sauté the shallots very gently and slowly until they start to caramelise, about 15-18 minutes. This low and slow method will enable the shallot to completely soften before browning.

4.  Transfer the caramelised shallots to a blender with the stock, roasted garlic, and remaining salt and pepper. Purée until smooth, then pour into a saucepan and bring to a simmer. Add the parmesan and cream, then continue to simmer until the soup is steaming, about 5 minutes.

5.  Divide the soup evenly between four bowls and sprinkle over the garlic croutons plus a little finely chopped fresh parsley. Enjoy!

# CHICKEN, BACON AND GARLIC TRAYBAKE

**PREPARATION TIME: 15 MINUTES | COOKING TIME: 1 HOUR | SERVES 4**

Whoever invented the mighty traybake deserves a medal, in my humble opinion. What's not to like about minimal preparation, tossing a load of ingredients into a roasting tin, and pretty much leaving it alone for 45 minutes or so? True to form, I've sneaked garlic into both the potatoes and the chicken: the result is absolutely delicious. Serve straight from the oven to the table and let everyone dive in and help themselves.

## INGREDIENTS

**For the chicken**

8 chicken thighs, bone in and skin on

2 tbsp oil

2 tsp finely minced garlic

1 tsp salt

1 tsp black pepper

½ tsp cayenne pepper

**For the potatoes**

1kg new potatoes, peeled (optional) and sliced to the thickness of a £1 coin

2 tbsp rapeseed oil

2 tsp finely minced garlic

1 tsp salt

½ tsp black pepper

**For the traybake**

6 banana shallots, peeled and halved lengthways

5 sprigs of oregano, leaves picked

1 lemon, sliced into wedges

5 garlic cloves, skins on

100g bacon lardons

75ml white wine

150ml chicken stock (made with 1 stock cube)

## METHOD

1. Preheat the oven to 190°c/170°c fan/gas mark 5.
   Make 3 deep slashes across the top of each chicken thigh to help them absorb the marinade, then place in a bowl with the remaining ingredients for the chicken. Turn the chicken thighs until they are fully coated in the seasoned oil. Set aside.

2. Place the potatoes in a bowl with the oil, garlic, salt and pepper. Turn the potatoes thoroughly until they are fully coated. Spread them out in a roasting tin and cook in the preheated oven for 20 minutes until they are starting to crisp up.

3. Meanwhile, heat a large frying pan with a tablespoon of oil. Place the marinated chicken in the pan, with a little distance between each piece (do this in two batches if necessary) and pan fry to seal the chicken thighs until lightly golden on both sides. Remove from the pan and set aside. Repeat with any remaining chicken thighs.

4. While the potatoes are cooking, prepare the shallots, oregano and lemon. Once the potatoes are done, lay the sealed chicken thighs on top of them in the roasting tin and scatter the shallots, oregano, lemon wedges, garlic cloves, and bacon lardons around them.

5. Return the tin to the oven for 20 minutes, then pour over the wine and stock. Cook for a final 20 minutes until the chicken is golden and cooked through.

# MUSSELS IN WHITE WINE SAUCE WITH GARLIC BUTTER TOASTS

**PREPARATION TIME: 15 MINUTES | COOKING TIME: 15 MINUTES | SERVES 4**

I simply had to include a recipe for mussels in this book, not just because they pair so beautifully with garlic but because they are an excellent source of protein, iron, selenium, iodine and omega-3, and low in saturated fat to boot! As if that wasn't enough, they are also cheap, and super quick and easy to cook, so that's a no brainer for me.

## INGREDIENTS

**For the garlic butter toasts**

40g unsalted butter

10g parmesan, grated

3 garlic cloves, peeled

1 tbsp chopped parsley leaves, plus extra to serve

½ tbsp tarragon leaves (or use extra parsley instead)

½ tsp smoked paprika

Large pinch of sea salt

4 slices of sourdough bread

**For the mussels**

1 tbsp olive oil

25g unsalted butter

25g parsley stalks, finely chopped (keep the leaves)

100g shallots, finely chopped (2 banana shallots)

4 whole garlic cloves, very thinly sliced

2-3 bay leaves

1 tsp paprika

½ tsp black pepper

300ml white wine

1kg mussels, cleaned and beards removed

1 lemon, quartered

## METHOD

1. For the garlic butter toasts, blitz all the ingredients except the sourdough in a food processor, then set aside. The butter can be made ahead and chilled in the fridge for up to a week.

2. For the mussels, heat the oil and butter over a medium heat in a large pan with a lid. Add the parsley stalks, shallots, sliced garlic, bay leaves, paprika, and black pepper. Sweat on a low heat for 5-6 minutes with the lid on until the shallots are softening and fragrant. Remove the lid and continue cooking until they develop a light golden hue.

3. Add the white wine to the pan, using a little more if you like lots of sauce, and cook for 2 minutes until simmering, then add the mussels. Stir well, ensuring the liquid gets into the mussels, then cover tightly with a lid and steam for 2-3 minutes until they have all opened.

4. Meanwhile, toast one side of each sourdough slice under the grill. Spread the other side thickly with the garlic butter and place back under the grill until the butter is bubbling. Turn off the grill and keep the toasts warm.

5. Spoon the mussels into bowls, pour over the pan juices, scatter with some chopped parsley and place the lemon quarters on top for squeezing over. Serve with the garlic butter toasts.

# PRAWNS IN GARLIC SAUCE (GAMBAS AL AJILLO)

**PREPARATION TIME: 20 MINUTES | COOKING TIME: 30 MINUTES | SERVES 4 AS PART OF A TAPAS MEAL**

In Spain this dish is made with garlic oil, garlic butter or garlic sauce using several different recipes depending on the region. The secret of this tasty tapas dish is the spicy stock that we extract from the prawn shells after peeling. We add this after frying the prawns and then leave it to simmer for a while to form a powerful sauce. You could use any size or type of shrimp for this recipe, such as scampi, langoustine or crayfish.

## INGREDIENTS

20 very large raw prawns with the shells on

2 tsp finely minced garlic

½ tsp sea salt or to taste

4 garlic cloves, very thinly sliced

1 medium-hot red chilli, thinly sliced

2 tbsp olive oil

1 tbsp lemon juice

2 tbsp finely chopped flat leaf parsley

Crusty bread, to serve

## METHOD

1. Peel the prawns, removing the heads and legs but leaving the tails on. Place the shells in a saucepan with the minced garlic and sea salt, then add just enough water to cover.

2. Simmer the prawn stock gently for about 10 minutes, then strain through a fine sieve into a clean jug or bowl and set aside.

3. While the stock is simmering, prepare the garlic cloves and chilli. Heat the olive oil in a frying pan and gently sauté the garlic and chilli on a low heat. We are trying to infuse the oil without burning the garlic, so cook it as low and slow as necessary until the garlic starts to turn slightly golden.

4. Add the prawn stock to the pan and simmer for 2-3 minutes. Add the prawns and simmer gently. As soon as the prawns start to show a little colour, stir in the lemon juice. Mix well and leave to simmer for another minute.

5. Garnish with the chopped parsley and serve with crusty bread.

# QUINOA SALAD WITH GARLIC LEMON DRESSING

**PREPARATION TIME: 20 MINUTES | COOKING TIME: 45 MINUTES | SERVES 4**

This salad is a feast for the eyes and the gut, using delicious ingredients that are roasted to bring out their sweetness, paired with garlic in both the marinade and the dressing. It also just happens to be gluten- and dairy-free, yet it delivers so much flavour and nutrition. Use up leftover roast vegetables or create your own favourite combination; try swapping the aubergine for pumpkin, sweet potato or cauliflower. For a nut-free option, swap the pine nuts for croutons.

## INGREDIENTS

**For the salad**

150g quinoa

300ml water or vegetable stock

4 tbsp olive oil

4 tsp finely minced garlic

1½ tsp black pepper

1½ tsp salt

3 large aubergines, cut into 2.5cm cubes

2 large or 3 medium peppers, cut into 2.5cm pieces

1 unwaxed lemon, sliced into 1cm rounds

2 tbsp pine nuts

50g rocket or mixed leaves

3 spring onions, thinly sliced

2 tbsp finely chopped flat leaf parsley

2 tbsp finely chopped fresh coriander

**For the dressing**

3 tsp finely minced garlic

3 tbsp extra virgin olive oil

2 tbsp lemon juice

1 tbsp honey

Salt and pepper, to taste

## METHOD

1. Toast the quinoa gently in a dry pan on a low heat for 4-5 minutes until beginning to smell nutty. Add the water or vegetable stock, bring to the boil and then lower the heat to cook with the lid on for 12 minutes. After 10 minutes, turn off the heat and allow the quinoa to finish cooking in its own steam. Transfer the quinoa to a bowl and fluff with a fork.

2. Preheat the oven to 200°c/180°c fan/gas mark 6. Line 2 large baking sheets with parchment. In a bowl, combine 2 tablespoons of olive oil with 3 teaspoons of minced garlic and 1 teaspoon each of salt and pepper, then add the aubergine and toss until coated. Spread out on the baking sheets and roast in the preheated oven for approximately 25-30 minutes until golden and soft. Remove and leave to cool.

3. Meanwhile, season the peppers with the remaining olive oil, garlic, salt and pepper. Transfer to the baking sheets and roast for 25-30 minutes until the skin is charred and soft.

4. Drizzle the lemon with 1 teaspoon of olive oil and a pinch of salt, then roast in the oven on the same tray as the peppers for 15-20 minutes until caramelised. Set aside to cool, then cut each round into quarters.

5. Meanwhile, roast the pine nuts in a dry frying pan until golden brown over a medium-low heat.

6. For the dressing, combine the ingredients in a bowl or jug. Whisk and then season to taste with salt and pepper.

7. To assemble the salad, combine the rocket, quinoa, roasted aubergine, pepper and lemon, spring onion, parsley, coriander, and pine nuts in a large bowl. Drizzle with the dressing and toss so the mixture is thoroughly combined.

8. Taste and season with additional salt and pepper if required, then let the salad sit for 10 minutes to absorb the dressing. Transfer to a large serving bowl or platter to serve.

# SAGE AND GARLIC SWEDE
# AND SWEET POTATO MASH

**PREPARATION TIME: 10 MINUTES | COOKING TIME: 20-25 MINUTES | SERVES 4**

Sage and garlic are happy bedfellows that elevate simple vegetables into something really warm, comforting and special. Swede and sweet potato mash is a great accompaniment to any number of dishes and makes a change from the usual carbs.

## INGREDIENTS

500g swede, peeled and cut into
1-2cm pieces

500g sweet potato, peeled and cut
into 2-3cm cubes

4 tbsp butter

1 tbsp finely chopped sage leaves

2 tsp finely minced garlic

150ml double cream

Salt and pepper, to taste

## METHOD

1.  Place the swede in a large saucepan, cover with water by a few inches and season generously with salt (at least 2 teaspoons). Bring to a boil, then reduce the heat to medium and cook for 5 minutes.

2.  Add the sweet potato and cook for a further 10 minutes, or until both that and the swede are easily pierced with the tip of a knife. Drain, reserving a little water, and set aside.

3.  Return the pan to the stove on a low to medium heat and add the butter. Once melted, add the sage and garlic to cook for 1 minute.

4.  Stir in the cream and bring it to a simmer, then remove from the heat. Return the swede and sweet potatoes to the pan, mash to the desired consistency and season with salt and pepper.

**Cook's Tip:** Make this up to two days ahead and keep refrigerated in an airtight container; the flavour just gets better.

# LAMB AND FETA BURGERS

**PREPARATION TIME: 1 HOUR 20 MINUTES | COOKING TIME: 12-14 MINUTES | SERVES 4**

Lamb, garlic, spices, and fresh herbs combine perfectly with the salty tang of feta cheese. I've been making this recipe since I can't remember when and it's always a big hit at barbecues. You can't beat a homemade burger, and this is a great dish to prepare ahead of time.

## INGREDIENTS

1 tbsp rapeseed oil

1 red onion, finely diced

3 garlic cloves, finely minced

400g lamb mince

100g feta, crumbled

50g soft white breadcrumbs

3 tbsp chopped coriander

3 tbsp chopped mint

1 lemon, zested

2 tsp harissa paste

1 tsp ground coriander

1 tsp smoked paprika

1 tsp ground cumin

1 tsp salt

**To serve**

4 brioche buns, toasted

Smoked garlic hummus dressing (see page 173)

Sliced tomatoes

Little gem lettuce leaves

## METHOD

1.  Heat the rapeseed oil in a frying pan, add the onion and cook gently over a low heat for 10 minutes or until softened. Add the garlic and cook for another minute. Set aside to cool.

2.  In a large mixing bowl, combine all the remaining ingredients along with the onion and garlic mixture and bring together with your hands ensuring that everything is well incorporated.

3.  Shape the mixture into 4 patties, cover with cling film and place in the fridge for half an hour to firm up.

4.  When ready to cook, heat a large frying pan over a medium heat and then add the burgers: you should hear a good sizzling sound. Cook the burgers for 1 minute, then turn the heat down to medium-low. Fry for a further 6 minutes on each side or until cooked through.

5.  Serve the burgers in toasted brioche buns, topped with smoked garlic hummus dressing, a slice or two of tomato and a couple of crunchy little gem leaves.

# TIGER PRAWNS IN TEQUILA

**PREPARATION TIME: 10 MINUTES | COOKING TIME: 10 MINUTES | SERVES 4**

Prawns are a fabulous get out of jail card in my house and I always keep a stash of tiger prawns around. Tequila may seem like an unusual paring, but it brings out the prawn flavour and adds depth like no other. This recipe is very simple and straightforward (my kind of food) and best served with soft fluffy rice to soak up the rich garlic butter sauce. Alternatively, you could serve them as a starter, or as a canapé without the sauce. However you serve them, they will be very well received!

## INGREDIENTS

24 shell-on tiger prawns, deveined (about 600g)

2 tbsp plain flour

1 tbsp paprika

1 tsp hot chilli powder (or cayenne pepper for a milder heat)

1 tsp garlic powder (or granules will work)

1 tsp salt

4 tbsp unsalted butter

4 cloves of garlic, finely chopped

2 tbsp tequila

1 tsp agave syrup

2 tbsp olive oil

1 lemon, halved

2 tbsp finely chopped fresh parsley

## METHOD

1. Start by cleaning the prawns and patting them dry. In a large bowl, combine the plain flour, paprika, chilli powder, garlic powder and salt. Mix well and then add the prawns, toss to coat them, and set aside.

2. In a large pan, melt the butter over a very low heat. Once melted, add the garlic and cook until aromatic and lightly golden which should take about 2-3 minutes. Now add the tequila and agave syrup and cook for 1-2 more minutes before pouring the sauce into a clean bowl.

3. Add the olive oil to the same pan and once warm, add the prawns in a single layer (cook in batches if the pan is too small). Cook them for about 2 minutes on each side, until nicely crisp and browned.

4. Pour the garlic butter sauce back into the pan and mix with the prawns. Cook for another minute but be careful not to overcook the prawns.

5. Season with salt and pepper to taste, then squeeze the fresh lemon juice all over the prawns. Garnish with the chopped parsley and serve with fluffy rice.

**Cook's Tip:** The prawns should be cooked as soon as they are coated, otherwise the coating could become claggy.

# WILD GARLIC AND RED ONION TART

**PREPARATION TIME: 20 MINUTES | COOKING TIME: 1 HOUR 30 MINUTES | SERVES 6**

Spring is the perfect time to forage for wild garlic, which can be found in the shady damp conditions of woodlands and forests; it's hard to miss because of its pungent garlicky aroma. It has a lighter flavour than garlic bulbs and can be eaten either raw or cooked. Wild garlic should be foraged responsibly by only taking what you need of the leaves, leaving the root intact for next year's crop.

## INGREDIENTS

1 pack of ready-rolled shortcrust pastry (320g)

Butter for greasing

2 tbsp olive oil

1 medium red onion, finely sliced into half moons

2 tsp finely minced garlic

1 large handful of wild garlic, stems finely chopped, leaves roughly chopped

350ml double cream

3 large eggs

1 tbsp + 1 tsp Dijon mustard

1 tsp salt

½ tsp freshly ground black pepper

100g extra mature cheddar, grated

## METHOD

1. Roll out the pastry to the thickness of a £1 coin. Grease a 24cm loose-based tart tin thoroughly with butter and then line with the pastry. Cover and refrigerate for 30 minutes.

2. While the pastry is resting, heat the oil in a frying pan over a gentle heat. Add the red onion and cook gently until softened and just starting to caramelise, then add the minced garlic and wild garlic stems. Cook for a further 5 minutes, then transfer the mixture to a bowl.

3. Put the frying pan back on the heat and cook the wild garlic leaves gently until just wilted. Remove from the heat and set aside. Preheat the oven to 200°c/180°c fan/gas mark 6.

4. Remove the pastry case from the refrigerator. Place a disk of baking parchment large enough to cover the sides into the pastry case and cover the bottom with baking beans.

5. Blind bake the pastry in the preheated oven for 15 minutes, then remove the paper and baking beans and cook for a further 5 minutes, or until the pastry looks dry and feels sandy to the touch. Turn the oven down to 150°c/130°c fan/gas mark 2.

6. Whisk the cream, eggs, teaspoon of mustard, salt, and pepper together in a jug. Brush the tablespoon of mustard over the base of the pastry case and sprinkle with half the cheddar. Now spread the onion mixture over the cheese, followed by the wild garlic leaves. Carefully pour the egg mixture into the pastry case, then sprinkle with the remaining cheese.

7. Bake the tart in the lower third of the oven for 40-50 minutes or until the filling is golden and set, with just a little wobble when shaken gently.

8. Let the tart cool a little before sliding it out of the tin and transferring to a cooling rack. Enjoy warm or chilled.

# GARLIC IN MIDDLE EASTERN CUISINE

Garlic is the backbone of Middle Eastern cookery and it's the countries that cluster around the Mediterranean Sea that use it most widely. Popular dips such as toum, hummus and baba ghanoush all feature garlic front and centre. Molokhia, the traditional Arab dish known as the food of the Pharaohs, contains an entire three bulbs of garlic!

Other than punchy, garlic-rich sauces, the key to Middle Eastern cuisine lies in its subtlety: the layering and blending of herbs and spices, the sweet and savoury accents, no single ingredient dominating. Garlic plays its part here too, cooked to melt unobtrusively and mingle with its fellow ingredients, but without it a dish is incomplete.

Middle Eastern cooks believe that you should take your time with garlic. Roasting rather than frying, mincing rather than chopping. They believe that garlic brings character to a dish and love the sweet mellow flavour of slow cooked garlic or the caramel hints of roasted garlic.

Meats, seafood and vegetables are lightly perfumed with garlic, whose fragrance perfectly complements the vast array of exotic spices that are so characteristic of Middle Eastern cuisine. No less than 25 countries constitute what we call the Middle East, more if you include North African countries such as Tunisia and Morocco. There is a commonality of ingredients at play here with garlic forming the backbone. This chapter merely scratches the surface but still manages to feature a selection of amazing dishes.

For me, the beauty of Middle Eastern cuisine is that it perfectly chimes with my mantra of not overcomplicating things. Sure, it features a host of delicious warming spices, a generous nod towards garlic, and of course a plethora of fresh herbs, yet there's nothing overly challenging in its preparation. My harissa lamb raan dish on the next page is a case in point: Super simple to prepare and insanely tasty. When you bring it to the table, nestled enticingly on a beautiful platter and dressed with a few simple garnishes, your guests will feel royally treated like the sultans and sultanas of old.

Vegetables and pulses come to life when paired with Middle Eastern seasonings. Even die-hard carnivores would be hard pushed to refuse seconds of my savoury butternut squash and chickpea baklava… it's simply that good! If you're trying to cut down on meat without compromising on flavour then check out my recipe for ful medames, the Egyptian breakfast staple, or my wickedly tasty cannellini beans with sweet paprika and garlic. You won't feel deprived of anything, I promise.

I hope I've inspired you to roll up your sleeves and don your apron to rustle up a Middle Eastern feast. Make like the tabbakhs (cooks) do and show garlic some love!

# GARLIC HARISSA LAMB RAAN

**PREPARATION TIME: 15 MINUTES, PLUS 1-2 HOURS MARINATING |
COOKING TIME: 3-3½ HOURS | SERVES 6**

There's very little preparation required for this dish yet the flavours are sensational. If you want to turn it into a showstopper, serve the lamb on a large platter and anoint it with pomegranate seeds, charred lemon halves, and coriander leaves. Smile sweetly as your guests gasp with admiration and remember, never ever tell them just how easy it is!

## INGREDIENTS

2 tsp black mustard seeds

5 tbsp Greek yoghurt

4 tbsp rose harissa

3 tsp finely minced garlic

1 tsp ground turmeric

1 tsp salt

1 tsp coarsely ground black pepper

1 unwaxed lime, zested and juiced

2kg leg of lamb, or shoulder if preferred

6-8 large garlic cloves

2 tbsp salted butter, melted

1-2 lemons, quartered

Pomegranate seeds

Coriander leaves

**Cook's Tip:** If you prefer the meat pink, reduce the overall cooking time by 1 hour and cook at 200°c/180°c fan/gas mark 6 without the foil balloon for the entire cooking time.

## METHOD

1. Line a large baking tray with parchment paper. Coarsely grind the mustard seeds with a mortar and pestle. Combine the ground mustard seeds with the yoghurt, harissa, minced garlic, turmeric, salt, pepper, lime zest, and lime juice. Mix to a smooth paste and adjust the seasoning with more salt and pepper to taste if needed.

2. Make incisions across the top and bottom of the lamb leg or shoulder, then insert the garlic cloves as deeply as possible. Massage the yoghurt marinade all over the lamb, then transfer to the baking tray and leave to marinate for 1-2 hours if possible, or refrigerate overnight.

3. Preheat the oven to 180°c/160°c fan/gas mark 4. When you're ready to cook the lamb, cover the tray with tin foil while leaving space around the lamb to create a balloon shape, then seal the edges tightly. Cook in the oven for about 2 hours 30 minutes until the meat is very tender and falling off the bone, basting the lamb with the melted butter after 2 hours.

4. After 2 hours 30 minutes, remove the tray from the oven, drain off some of the liquid and reserve for later. Turn the oven temperature up to 200°c/180°fan/gas mark 6. Baste the lamb with butter once again, place the quartered lemons in the tray, then return it to the oven and cook uncovered for a further 30-40 minutes at the higher temperature.

5. Remove the tray from the oven, leave in a warm place and cover once more to let the joint rest before serving. Baste the lamb with the butter again for a final glaze.

6. While the lamb is resting, reheat the reserved juices and serve as a jus for the lamb. To dress the lamb, scatter some pomegranate seeds and fresh coriander over the platter.

# CHICKEN SHISH KEBAB WITH GARLIC SAUCE

**PREPARATION TIME: 1 HOUR 15 MINUTES, INCLUDING MARINATING | COOKING TIME: 15 MINUTES | SERVES 4**

Kebabs often get a bad rap due to their perception as a greasy snack following a night in the pub! However, a freshly made kebab enrobed in a fluffy wrap and filled with crunchy fresh salad, garlic and chilli sauce and tangy pickles is a thing of beauty, and healthy too. The acidity of the tomato in the marinade helps to tenderise the chicken and the sugars give it a glorious golden colour as it cooks. You'll need some wooden skewers for this recipe too.

## INGREDIENTS

**For the kebab**

500g chicken thigh fillets, cubed

1 red pepper, cubed (slightly smaller than the chicken pieces)

2 tbsp olive oil

**For the marinade**

3 tbsp natural yoghurt

2 tbsp olive oil

1 tbsp tomato purée

3 tsp finely minced garlic

½ lemon, zested and juiced

2 tsp ground cumin

1 tsp Aleppo chilli flakes (pul biber)

1 tsp sweet smoked paprika

½ tsp black pepper and ¼ tsp salt

**For the garlic sauce**

6 tbsp natural yoghurt

2 tsp finely minced garlic

½ a lemon, zested

**To serve**

Pitta or flatbreads

2 baby gem lettuces

2 small tomatoes, sliced

1 small red onion, finely sliced

Pickles of your choice

## METHOD

1. Start by mixing all the ingredients for the garlic sauce together in a bowl, with salt and pepper to taste, then set aside.

2. Now combine all the ingredients for the marinade in another bowl. Massage the marinade into the chicken and pepper chunks, making sure they are generously coated. Set aside to marinate for an hour or refrigerate overnight.

3. Meanwhile, soak the wooden skewers in water for at least 30 minutes. Thread a piece of marinated chicken onto a skewer followed by a piece of pepper, then repeat until you have 4 pieces of chicken and 4 pieces of pepper on each skewer. Don't squash them together if the skewer isn't long enough.

4. When you are ready to cook, heat the olive oil in a frying pan over a low heat. Cook the kebabs for approximately 6-7 minutes on each side or until slightly charred and cooked through.

5. Pile the chicken and peppers into pitta or flatbread with plenty of salad, garlic sauce and pickles.

# BUTTERNUT SQUASH AND CHICKPEA BAKLAVA

**PREPARATION TIME: 40 MINUTES | COOKING TIME: 1 HOUR 20 MINUTES | SERVES 6**

Who says baklava has to be sweet? This savoury vegetarian take on the classic pastry is so moreish, even carnivores will have to be beaten back as they reach for another slice! Served hot or cold, the baklava is delicious on its own or you could add an interesting salad to turn it into a satisfying main meal.

## INGREDIENTS

1kg butternut squash (peeled weight), peeled and diced into 1cm cubes

4 tbsp olive oil (2 tbsp for the squash, 2 tbsp for the filling)

400g tinned chickpeas, drained and rinsed

2 tsp cumin seeds

2 tbsp harissa

2 onions, finely chopped

1 leek, white part chopped

3 tsp finely minced garlic

180g cooked and peeled chestnuts, chopped

150g soft white breadcrumbs

Handful of coriander, finely chopped

50g sultanas

100ml vegetable stock

2 x 270g packs of filo pastry

75g unsalted butter, melted

200g feta, crumbled

1 tsp black onion seeds

Drizzle of runny honey

Pinch of dried chilli flakes

Sea salt flakes

## METHOD

1. Preheat the oven to 200°c/180°c fan/gas mark 6. Put the diced squash on a baking tray, drizzle with 2 tablespoons of the olive oil, season generously with salt and pepper, then toss to coat all the cubes. Bake for 10 minutes.

2. Transfer the squash to a large bowl and add the chickpeas, cumin seeds and harissa. Stir everything together, spread out on the tray and return to the oven to cook for a further 15 minutes or until the squash is just tender. Leave to cool.

3. Turn the oven down to 180°c/160°c/gas mark 4. Heat the remaining olive oil in a pan and cook the onions, leek and garlic for 10-15 minutes over a low heat until softened.

4. Put half the onion mixture in a bowl with the chestnuts, breadcrumbs, coriander, sultanas and stock. Mix and season. Stir the remaining onion mixture into the squash and chickpeas.

5. To assemble the baklava, trim the filo sheets so they fit neatly into a deep 25cm x 35cm baking dish or roasting tin. Brush the dish with melted butter. Brush 4 of the filo sheets with melted butter, then layer them up in the bottom of the dish. Add a third of the squash mix, a third of the chestnut mix and a third of the crumbled feta.

6. Top with another 4 sheets of buttered filo and add another third of each mixture. Top with another 4 sheets of filo, then the remaining mixture, then finish with a final layer of 4 sheets.

7. Cut a classic baklava pattern into the pastry all the way through to the bottom layer. Sprinkle with the onion seeds, then bake for 30-40 minutes or until the baklava is deep golden and crisp. Cool for 10 minutes in the dish.

8. Drizzle the baklava with honey and sprinkle with chilli flakes and salt before serving in wedges. A dollop of Turkish chilli sauce (see page 177) makes a great accompaniment.

# GARLIC AND HERB FLATBREADS

**PREPARATION TIME: 10 MINUTES | COOKING TIME: 10-15 MINUTES | MAKES 2 LARGE FLATBREADS**

No self-respecting Middle Eastern table would be complete without a bread of some sort. As these flatbreads don't contain yeast, they don't need time to prove so they're really quick and easy to make. The addition of the yoghurt gives them a lovely chewy texture and a bit of tang.

## INGREDIENTS

200g self-raising flour

1 tsp baking powder

125g natural yoghurt

½ tsp dried oregano

1 tsp caraway seeds

1 tsp salt

A little oil

50g butter

4 garlic cloves, grated

Handful of flat leaf parsley, roughly chopped

½ tsp sea salt

## METHOD

1. Place the flour, baking powder, yoghurt, oregano, caraway seeds, and salt in a mixing bowl. Mix to form a soft sticky dough.

2. Turn the dough out onto a lightly floured surface and knead gently for 1 minute. Divide the dough into two pieces and roll each piece into a circle approximately 5mm thick and 24cm wide.

3. Place a large non-stick pan over a high heat. Wipe the pan with a little oil on some kitchen paper to lightly grease it.

4. Cook the flatbreads in batches for 2-3 minutes on each side. They should bubble up as they cook. Wrap the cooked flatbreads in a clean tea towel or cover with foil to keep them warm.

5. Meanwhile, melt the butter in a small frying pan or saucepan over a low-medium heat. Remove from the heat, add the grated garlic and parsley to warm through in the residual heat, then season with a good pinch of sea salt.

6. Gently score the top of the warm flatbreads and then spoon over the garlic butter.

# BAHARAT
# SPICED CHICKEN

**PREPARATION TIME: 10 MINUTES | COOKING TIME: 50 MINUTES | SERVES 4**

As you might know by now, I try to avoid complicated cooking like the plague and this gorgeous dish is both delicious and an absolute doddle to make. Roasted fennel would make a great accompaniment, as would my roasted potatoes with preserved lemon (see page 112). Here I've used chicken legs as they're inexpensive but very tasty and filling. Of course, you could substitute these with chicken thighs or even a whole chicken come to that.

## INGREDIENTS

4 chicken legs, bone in and skin on

1 tbsp baharat spice blend

2 tbsp rapeseed oil

Sea salt

250ml chicken stock

**For the marinade**

2 tbsp rapeseed oil

1 tbsp natural yoghurt

3 tsp finely minced garlic

2 tsp rose harissa paste

1 tsp hot smoked paprika

1 lemon, zested

1 tsp honey

½ tsp salt

## METHOD

1. Preheat the oven to 200°c/180°c fan/gas mark 6. Rub the chicken legs all over with the baharat spice and set aside.

2. Make the marinade by mixing all the ingredients together in a bowl. Set aside.

3. Heat the rapeseed oil in a frying pan on a medium heat. Season the spiced chicken legs with a little sea salt and fry for about 5 minutes on each side until golden brown all over. You may have to do this in batches.

4. Transfer the chicken legs to a roasting tin and pour the stock around them. Spoon the marinade over the chicken legs and brush to coat them well.

5. Cover the roasting tin with foil and cook in the preheated oven for 30 minutes. Remove the foil and roast the chicken for a further 10-15 minutes or until cooked through, golden and crispy. Serve with some of the roasting tin juices spooned over the meat.

# CANNELLINI BEANS WITH SWEET PAPRIKA AND GARLIC

**PREPARATION TIME: 15 MINUTES, PLUS 12 HOURS SOAKING |**
**COOKING TIME: 2 HOURS 30 MINUTES | SERVES 4**

This is a delicious and hearty vegetarian dish with a lingering smoky sweetness from the paprika. Beans are an excellent source of fibre, folate, iron, and magnesium, plus they are high in protein which will keep you fuller for longer. The warm beans are finished with a garlicky, oniony oil which they soak up eagerly.

## INGREDIENTS

500g dried cannellini beans

1 tsp salt

1 onion, roughly chopped

1 medium tomato, roughly chopped

1 large carrot, cut into chunks

3 celery stalks, cut into chunks

4 garlic cloves, bruised

4 bay leaves

3 sprigs of thyme

Handful of parsley stems

2 tsp smooth mustard

**To finish**

4 tbsp olive oil

1 large onion, diced (150g)

1 tsp salt

2 garlic cloves, finely minced

2 tbsp sweet paprika

1 tsp black pepper

½ tsp cayenne pepper

## METHOD

1.  Rinse the beans in a colander, then put them in a large bowl, cover with plenty of cold water and leave them on the counter overnight.

2.  The next day, drain and rinse the beans, then transfer them to a large saucepan, cover with fresh water by a couple of inches and put on a high heat. Add the salt, prepared vegetables, garlic cloves, and herbs.

3.  Bring to the boil, then lower the heat to a simmer and skim off any foam with a ladle. Taste the water for salt, add more if needed, and cook until the beans are very tender but not falling apart. Stir infrequently but check often and add water as needed. They will take anywhere from 1-2 hours, depending on the beans. Taste 5 or 6 beans to be sure that they are all fully cooked and not at all chalky.

4.  Remove any large vegetables or aromatics from the pot, leaving the beans in their liquid. Add the mustard of your choice and stir through. (You can reserve the vegetables and eat separately if you like – they are full of goodness too.)

5.  To finish the dish, heat the oil in a pan over a low heat. Add the diced onions and salt to sauté with the lid on, stirring occasionally, for about 15 minutes or until the onion is very tender and just slightly coloured. Add the garlic, stir well and cook for about 30 seconds, until it turns fragrant but doesn't colour at all. Add the paprika and cook for another minute.

6.  If the beans are underwater, pour off the excess liquid into a separate container (save it for soup, adding the reserved cooked vegetables) so the beans are only partially covered.

7.  Stir the beans into the onion mixture, season with black pepper and cayenne, then serve with lightly toasted sourdough bread. Enjoy!

# CHICKEN TAGINE WITH DATES AND ALMONDS

**PREPARATION TIME: 15 MINUTES | COOKING TIME: 1 HOUR 15 MINUTES | SERVES 4**

Deep, delicious and divine is the only way to describe the flavours in this recipe. For a dish that yields so much intensity one could easily imagine you'd laboured over it for days, when in fact it's a one-pot dish. Although it's called a tagine, I've never actually made it in a tagine, though I have used a slow cooker and had amazing results every time.

## INGREDIENTS

4 tbsp oil

600g chicken thighs, boned and cut into 4 pieces (or chicken breast if preferred)

2 cinnamon sticks

1 large onion, finely diced

5 small whole garlic cloves

2 tsp finely minced garlic

2 tsp Hungarian paprika

2 tsp roasted ground cumin

2 tsp ground coriander

1 tsp ground cinnamon

1 tsp ground turmeric

½ tsp salt, or to taste

¼ tsp hot chilli powder

¼ tsp grated nutmeg

400ml chicken stock

40g pitted dates

20g blanched whole almonds

Large pinch of chopped fresh coriander

## METHOD

1. Heat 1 tablespoon of the oil in a large sauté pan with a lid. Place the chicken into the pan, uncovered, and seal the outside edges until each piece of chicken is golden, but not cooked through. Cook in batches to ensure you don't crowd the pan when sealing and glazing, as this will prevent the chicken from boiling and help it to caramelise instead. Remove from the pan and set aside, leaving any remaining oil in the pan.

2. Add the remaining oil to the pan with the cinnamon sticks, onion, and whole garlic cloves. Cook on a low heat until they have all softened.

3. Stir in the minced garlic, paprika, ground cumin, coriander, cinnamon, and turmeric, salt, chilli powder, and nutmeg. Cook for 5 minutes on a low heat so that the flavours infuse and become aromatic.

4. Now add the chicken stock, dates and almonds to the pan. Bring the liquid to a simmer for 2-3 minutes before returning the chicken to the pan along with any resting juices. Simmer on a low heat with the lid on for 40-45 minutes, stirring only occasionally. The aim is to cook the chicken very slowly so that it melts in the mouth. Check the level of sauce in the pan from time to time to ensure that it hasn't thickened too much, adding a little hot water to loosen the consistency if necessary.

5. Remove the pan from the heat and garnish the tagine with fresh coriander, then serve with pilaf rice on the side.

**Cook's Tip:** If you don't usually use salt in your cooking, add it to taste at the end of the cooking time, as the salt level in stock cubes can vary so the dish may be seasoned enough from the chicken stock.

# GRILLED HARISSA SEABASS WITH SMOKED GARLIC BUTTER

**PREPARATION TIME: 10 MINUTES | COOKING TIME: 10 MINUTES | SERVES 4**

Widely used in North African cuisine, harissa paste imparts chilli heat with a wonderful depth of flavour that includes garlic, citrus and smoky notes. The smoky garlic butter adds an elegant finishing touch to this deceptively simple dish. Seabass is a wonderful fish full of protein, great for your heart and brain health, and so easy to digest. If you don't want to cook a whole fish, you can easily use fillets without any compromise on flavour.

## INGREDIENTS

**For the bass and broccoli**

2 whole large seabass, scaled and gutted (around 850g-1kg)

4 tsp harissa paste

2 garlic cloves, thinly sliced

1 lemon, sliced into 0.5cm thick rounds

1 tsp flaky sea salt

300g tenderstem broccoli

Drizzle of rapeseed oil

**For the smoked garlic butter**

50g butter, softened

3 tbsp chopped coriander

1 tbsp Bart's smoked garlic paste (or normal black garlic paste)

1 lemon, zested

¼ tsp ground cumin

¼ tsp flaky sea salt

## METHOD

1.  Wash and clean the bass, then pat dry with kitchen paper. Lightly score the skin of the fish at 1cm intervals on both sides, then rub the harissa into the flesh and inside the cavity. Place the fish on baking tray, then tuck the sliced garlic and lemon into the cavity and around the fish. Sprinkle with the sea salt and set aside.

2.  Plunge the broccoli into a pan of boiling water, put the lid on and blanch for 2-3 minutes. Drain the broccoli and plunge into a bowl of iced water to stop it cooking and retain the fresh green colour. Set aside.

3.  Turn on the grill or heat up a barbecue. Stir the chopped coriander, black garlic, lemon zest, ground cumin, and sea salt into the softened butter. Add a teaspoon of this mixture to the cavity of the prepared fish and spread another teaspoon on top.

4.  Grill or barbecue the fish for 6-8 minutes on each side until the skin is crisp and starting to char. The fillet will lift away easily from the bone when it's cooked.

5.  While the fish cooks, place a frying pan over a high heat. Once smoking hot, add the broccoli with a very small dash of oil and a knob of the smoked garlic butter. Char the broccoli for a few minutes on both sides until warmed through with crispy charred spears. You can also cook this on the barbecue if desired.

6.  Once everything is ready, serve the grilled fish and charred broccoli with a green salad.

**Cook's Tip:** If it's difficult to find large seabass, you can buy 4 individual fish instead – just be aware that you may need to adjust the ingredient quantities a little.

# ROAST POTATOES WITH PRESERVED LEMON, GARLIC AND CHILLI

**PREPARATION TIME: 25 MINUTES | COOKING TIME: 35 MINUTES | SERVES 6**

This recipe contains four of my favourite ingredients: garlic, potatoes, chillies and preserved lemons – I'm in heaven with this dish! The salty, tangy preserved lemon plays two parts here: it's roasted in the same pan as the potatoes along with garlic, jalapeño and red onion, and it's also used to ramp up the parsley and mint salad that's sprinkled on just before serving.

## INGREDIENTS

2kg Maris Piper potatoes

2 tsp salt

5 tbsp oil, plus a little extra

3 tsp finely minced garlic

½ tsp coarsely ground black pepper

1 bulb of garlic, cloves separated and pressed to slightly open, with the skins still on

1 preserved lemon, sliced and quartered

1 jalapeño chilli, finely sliced

1 red onion, thinly sliced

10 parsley strands, leaves finely chopped

20 mint leaves, finely sliced

1 tsp lemon juice

## METHOD

1. Preheat the oven to 200°c/180°c fan/gas mark 6. Peel and cut the potatoes into 2.5cm cubes, then place them in a large pan. Cover with water by 5cm and add the salt. Bring to the boil, then reduce the heat and simmer until just tender when pierced with the tip of a knife and fluffy if lightly bashed, which should take 6-8 minutes. Drain and pat dry.

2. In a large bowl, combine 4 tablespoons of the oil with the minced garlic, the black pepper and 2 or 3 good pinches of salt. Mix well, then add the potatoes and toss to coat.

3. Transfer the potatoes to a baking tray and spread out so they are not touching each other. Roast in the preheated oven, turning occasionally, until golden brown and crisp, which should take about 35 minutes. Don't wash up the bowl yet!

4. Add the garlic cloves to the same bowl you used for the potatoes, drizzle in a little oil and mix to coat the cloves.

5. When the potatoes have been roasting for 25 minutes, add the garlic cloves to the tray and return it to the oven for the next 10 minutes.

6. Meanwhile, put most of the preserved lemon into the same bowl (reserving a quarter for the garnish) along with the sliced jalapeño and red onion. Add the remaining tablespoon of oil and mix well.

7. After the initial 35 minutes, remove the potatoes from the oven, scatter the onion mixture over the top and cook for about 8-10 minutes until the onions are golden and lightly crispy, and the preserved lemons are cooked and crunchy.

8. Meanwhile, toss the parsley, mint, remaining lemons and lemon juice in a bowl, then season with salt and pepper to taste.

9. When the potatoes are ready, transfer to the serving dish and scatter the herb salad on top.

# FUL MEDAMES

**PREPARATION TIME: 15 MINUTES | COOKING TIME: 40 MINUTES | SERVES 4 AS A SIDE**

Ful medames is traditionally a stew of cooked broad beans, commonly eaten for breakfast in Egyptian and Lebanese households. Frankly though it's good at any time of the day, especially when enjoyed with a few freshly cooked flatbreads to mop up the delicious juices. If broad beans are not in season, just use frozen broad beans as I have in this recipe; they have a lovely flavour and texture, and their bright green hue really brings the dish to life. Don't be concerned by the amount of olive oil, it really aids digestion in bean dishes so is an essential ingredient here.

## INGREDIENTS

650g frozen baby broad beans

5 tbsp olive oil

100g onion, finely diced

3 tsp finely minced garlic

2 tsp sea salt flakes

2 tsp ground cumin

1 tsp chilli flakes

2 large tomatoes, diced

2 tbsp lemon juice

½ tsp ground black pepper

4 tbsp chopped flat leaf parsley leaves

## METHOD

1. Bring a saucepan of salted water to the boil. Add the beans and simmer for 2 minutes. Drain, retaining the cooking liquid, and then pop the beans out of their skins once cooled.

2. Heat 3 tablespoons of the olive oil in a frying pan and gently fry the onion and garlic for 5 minutes.

3. Add the salt, cumin, chilli flakes, and diced tomatoes to the frying pan. Cook over a very low heat for 30 minutes. Add some of the bean cooking liquid if the mixture seems dry.

4. Stir the podded broad beans, lemon juice and black pepper into the tomato sauce and simmer gently for 2 minutes.

5. Finish the dish with chopped parsley and the remaining olive oil drizzled over the top.

# GREEN LENTIL STEW WITH ROASTED GARLIC

**PREPARATION TIME: 10 MINUTES | COOKING TIME: 1 HOUR 15 MINUTES | SERVES 4**

Wait! Before you skip over this page, let me entice you to make this recipe which features among my top five favourite lentil dishes thanks to the deep, smoky, garlicky, sassy flavours. It's everything you would associate with the magic of North African cuisine and for those of you who like hearty recipes, this dish gives you everything and more. If you did want to add meat, it's so easy to drop in some cooked leftovers from another meal.

## INGREDIENTS

300g dried green lentils

2 fat bulbs of garlic

600ml water

2-3 large bay leaves

3 sage leaves or ½ tsp dried sage

2 tsp chopped fresh oregano or 1 tsp dried oregano

3 tbsp olive oil

1 tsp cumin seeds

1 red onion, finely diced (120g)

1 medium carrot, finely diced (200g)

1 large red pepper, diced into 1cm cubes

1 tsp cayenne pepper

1 tsp sweet paprika

1 tsp smoked paprika

1 tsp black pepper

1½ tsp salt

400g potatoes, diced into 0.5cm cubes

300g passata

2 tsp red wine vinegar

2 tbsp pomegranate molasses

1 tbsp chopped fresh coriander or parsley

## METHOD

1. Wash the lentils and soak them for 30 minutes, time permitting. Preheat the oven to 180°c/160°c fan/gas mark 4. Wrap the garlic bulbs in damp parchment paper and roast them for 45 minutes. Once cooled, squeeze the garlic out of the skins and mash it up using a fork.

2. Meanwhile, put the lentils, water, bay leaves, sage, and oregano in a large saucepan. Bring to the boil, reduce the heat, and simmer for about 20 minutes, or until the lentils are tender. Remove the bay leaves.

3. Gently heat the oil in a large saucepan, add the cumin seeds, allow them to crackle for a few seconds, then stir in the red onion. Cook on a low heat with the lid on until the onion has softened but not coloured (this should take about 10-12 minutes). Add the carrot and red pepper to cook until tender.

4. Now add the cayenne pepper, sweet and smoked paprika, black pepper, and salt to the vegetables. Cook for a few minutes, then stir in the diced potatoes, passata, and roasted mashed garlic. Cook for 15 minutes at a medium-low heat until it's bubbling away.

5. Combine the lentils and their cooking liquid with the vegetables and red wine vinegar, season as required with salt and pepper, then cook over a low heat for 20 minutes with the lid on. If needed, add boiling water to achieve the consistency you prefer.

6. Just before serving the stew, add the pomegranate molasses and stir through to combine. Sprinkle with the fresh coriander and get ready to be surprised!

# BUTTER BEAN AND PARSLEY DIP WITH PITTA CRISPS

**PREPARATION TIME: 10 MINUTES | COOKING TIME: 6-8 MINUTES | SERVES 2-4**

This recipe is about simplicity and easy eating. Don't be concerned by the amount of olive oil used with the butter beans; good oils will help you digest pulses and lubricate your joints. The liberal use of parsley adds a boost of vitamin C, iron, potassium, magnesium, and fibre.

## INGREDIENTS

**For the pitta crisps**

2 large wholemeal pitta breads

2 tsp finely chopped garlic

½ tsp black pepper

¼ tsp salt

1 tbsp olive oil

1 sprig of rosemary (optional)

**For the butter bean dip**

2-3 handfuls of parsley (10-15 sprigs, coarse stalks removed)

3 fat garlic cloves

1 tbsp lemon juice, or to taste

1 tsp ground cumin

½ - ¾ tsp salt

½ tsp black pepper, or to taste

4 tbsp olive oil, or to taste

400g tinned butter beans, drained and rinsed

## METHOD

1. Preheat the oven to 180°c/160°c fan/gas mark 4. Cut the pitta breads into 1cm strips and combine the garlic, black pepper, salt and olive oil in a small bowl.

2. Brush the garlicky oil over the pitta strips and spread them out on a non-stick baking tray. Add the rosemary if using. Place in the oven for 6-8 minutes until very lightly browned.

3. Meanwhile, make the dip by placing the parsley, garlic, lemon juice, cumin, salt, and black pepper into a food processor. Add half the olive oil and blitz until smoothly blended.

4. Now add half the butter beans and remaining olive oil to the food processor, then blitz once again until you have a smooth consistency. Taste and season the dip accordingly, making sure the flavours are evenly blended throughout. Extra lemon juice will really enhance the flavour.

5. Transfer the butter bean dip to small serving bowls, drizzle a little olive oil over the top, garnish with a parsley leaf and serve with the pitta crisps.

# ROASTED AUBERGINE WITH SPICED RICE

**PREPARATION TIME: 15 MINUTES | COOKING TIME: 30 MINUTES | SERVES 4**

Aubergines are a staple vegetable in my home, and I cook with them in several ways, particularly in my Indian dishes. However, this recipe waited patiently in my subconscious for quite some time before it could percolate properly, and has now been brought together with my spiced rice. Should you have leftovers – and I always ensure I do – you can quite easily turn it into a light lunch the next day, when it tastes even better.

## INGREDIENTS

4 small aubergines, cut into 2cm rounds (800g)

6 tbsp olive oil

6 garlic cloves, sliced thinly

1 tsp sea salt

1 tsp black pepper

1 tbsp finely chopped fresh flat leaf parsley

1 tbsp finely chopped fresh mint

1 tbsp extra virgin olive oil

**For the spiced rice**

300g basmati rice, washed

30g ghee or butter

3 cardamom pods, bruised

½ cinnamon stick

1 medium onion (150g), finely chopped

3 garlic cloves, finely minced

1 tsp ground cumin

½ tsp salt

½ tsp black pepper

600ml vegetable stock

40g roasted pine nuts

2 tbsp chopped coriander

## METHOD

1. Preheat the oven to 220°c/200°c fan/gas mark 7. Soak the rice in warm water while you prepare the aubergine. Gently heat 2 tablespoons of the oil in a large frying pan, add the sliced garlic and cook for 2-3 minutes on a very low heat without colouring, then scoop out and set aside.

2. Place the aubergine rounds into the frying pan, making sure the cut side is flat on the surface (you may need to do this in batches), and cook until lightly golden brown on both sides. Aubergine absorbs a lot of oil, so add a little more if needed.

3. Transfer the browned aubergine to a baking sheet and sprinkle with salt and pepper, then bake in the oven for about 20-25 minutes or until tender, golden and crispy around the edges.

4. Meanwhile, melt the ghee or butter in a medium saucepan and add the cardamom pods and cinnamon stick, quickly followed by the onion. Stir well to coat the onion and cook without browning until softened and beginning to develop a golden hue.

5. Add the garlic to the saucepan and cook for 1 minute until aromatic, then add the drained rice, ground cumin, salt, and black pepper. Stir to coat the rice in the seasonings and cook for 1-2 minutes until the rice is dry frying.

6. Stir in the stock, bring to a simmer and cook with the lid on for 12 minutes or until the liquid has been absorbed. Remove the pan from the heat and let it stand, covered, for a further 10 minutes. Stir in the pine nuts and fresh coriander.

7. When the aubergine is cooked, remove it from the oven, season to taste with more salt and pepper, scatter the fried garlic slices on top, garnish with the fresh parsley and mint, then drizzle with the extra virgin olive oil to finish. Serve with the spiced rice and perhaps a yoghurt dip on the side.

# ROASTED GARLIC AND BAHARAT SPICED FOCACCIA

**PREPARATION TIME: 15 MINUTES | COOKING TIME: 40 MINUTES | SERVES 4-6**

I've put a Persian twist on my favourite bread, the noble focaccia. The word baharat simply means spice, and the ingredients vary but usually include a gorgeous blend of coriander seeds, cumin seeds, cloves, black peppercorns, green cardamom, nutmeg, and paprika. If you haven't made bread before this is a great entry level recipe, although I must warn you that making bread can become addictive!

## INGREDIENTS

**For the focaccia**

2 bulbs of garlic

500g 00 flour (pasta flour)

1 tbsp baharat spice mix

1 tbsp caster sugar

4g fast-acting dried yeast

400ml warm water

2 tbsp olive oil

10g fine salt

Sea salt

**For the garlic butter**

4 garlic cloves, finely minced

30g unsalted butter, melted

1 tbsp olive oil

1 tsp ground cumin

½ tsp pul biber chilli flakes

## METHOD

1. Preheat the oven to 180°c/160°c/gas mark 4. Drizzle the garlic bulbs with oil, wrap loosely in tin foil, place on a baking tray and bake for 40 minutes. Unwrap and leave to cool, then pop the roasted garlic cloves out of their skins.

2. In a large bowl, combine the flour, spices, sugar and yeast. Add 300ml of warm water and mix using a spoon or cutlery knife. Add the remaining water with the olive oil and fine salt, then mix the dough until no dry spots remain. Cover and leave in a warm place for 30 minutes (the airing cupboard is ideal).

3. With oiled hands, gently lift and fold one side of the dough. Turn the bowl and repeat until the dough becomes smoother and you can feel a little resistance. Cover and leave somewhere warm for 1-2 hours or until doubled in size.

4. Brush a baking tray liberally with olive oil. Oil your hands and perform another series of lifts and folds until the dough feels smooth again and tauter. Lift the dough into the oiled tray and perform a few more lifts and folds. Rub some oil on top of the dough, cover and leave to double in size for 40 minutes.

5. Preheat the oven to 220°c/200°c fan/gas mark 7. Gently push the dough into the corners of the tray and then press your fingers in at regular intervals to create dimples. Push the roasted garlic cloves into the dimples, drizzle oil generously over the top and then sprinkle with sea salt. Bake in the oven for 20-25 minutes until golden and risen. Cool in the tin for 10 minutes and then turn out onto a wire rack.

6. For the garlic butter, combine all the ingredients in a small pan over a medium heat, cook for 1 minute until the garlic is lightly browned, then transfer to a bowl and season to taste.

7. Once the focaccia is out of the oven, spread the garlic butter all over it with a spoon. Cool before slicing and serving.

# TUNISIAN FISH STEW WITH NEW POTATOES

**PREPARATION TIME: 10 MINUTES | COOKING TIME: 45 MINUTES | SERVES 4**

My fish stew, while headlining Tunisian inspiration, could appear on any Mediterranean or Persian plate. It's a simple yet elegant dish with a little twist, providing a generous helping of goodness from fish, fresh herbs and spices that make it flavoursome without being overly complicated. I would recommend any white fish such as haddock, hake, cod or coley.

## INGREDIENTS

200g ripe tomatoes

2 tbsp olive oil

4 large garlic cloves, finely sliced

2 tsp harissa paste

2 tsp paprika

1 tsp ground cumin

½ tsp cayenne pepper

250g new potatoes

500ml light fish stock or water

500g white fish fillets, skin on and cut into 2.5cm chunks

Handful of flat leaf parsley or coriander, chopped

3-4 sprigs of mint, destalked and chopped

½ a lemon, juiced

1 tsp sea salt

## METHOD

1. Start by blanching the tomatoes: plunge them into boiling water for 2 minutes, then transfer to a sealable bag. Leave to rest for a few minutes and the skin should easily peel off. Once peeled, cut the tomatoes into 1cm cubes.

2. Heat the oil in a wide heavy-based pan, add the garlic and sauté for 2-3 minutes on a very low temperature to ensure it doesn't burn. Now add the diced tomatoes and cook for 7-8 minutes on a gentle heat.

3. Add the harissa paste and dry spices, stir through, then cook for 2-3 minutes to allow the flavours to release and meld into the tomatoes.

4. Add the potatoes and cook for 10 minutes on a gentle heat to enable them to absorb all the flavours before adding the fish stock or water. Give the mixture a stir and increase the heat to a rapid simmer. Turn the heat back down and simmer on a low heat for about 20-25 minutes or until the potatoes are tender.

5. Add the fish, stir through, and simmer for another 4-5 minutes or until the fish is cooked. Fold in the fresh herbs, lemon juice and salt. Adjust the seasoning to taste and serve.

# VEGETABLE PILAF
# WITH APRICOTS

**PREPARATION TIME: 15 MINUTES | COOKING TIME: 40 MINUTES | SERVES 4**

I think this has to be my favourite rice dish, bar none. Heady with garlic, sweet from the apricots and unctuous from the ghee, it's a worthy accompaniment to any number of Middle Eastern dishes, particularly tagines. It also pairs rather well with Indian curries so is a super versatile dish to have in your arsenal.

## INGREDIENTS

300g basmati rice

3 tbsp ghee

2 garlic cloves, thinly sliced

2 cinnamon sticks

1 medium onion, thinly sliced

2 tsp finely minced garlic

1 tsp ground cumin

½ tsp ground coriander

¼ tsp ground turmeric

1 tsp salt

1 tbsp finely chopped dried apricots

600ml vegetable stock

60g garden peas

Chopped fresh coriander, to taste

## METHOD

1. Start by washing the rice in a bowl of warm water until the water runs clear – you may need to wash the rice with 3-4 changes of water. Once you have rinsed the rice, put it into a bowl of cold water and leave to soak for 15 minutes. Drain when ready to use.

2. Melt the ghee in a large pan and when warm, add the thinly sliced garlic and sauté for 1-2 minutes on a low heat. When the garlic is lightly golden, remove it from the pan and set aside.

3. Now add the cinnamon sticks to the garlic-infused oil, followed by the onion, minced garlic, ground spices and salt. Cook until the onions are soft.

4. Add the apricots and the washed rice to the pan. Stir until the rice is coated in the spices and cook for 5-6 minutes.

5. Now add the stock, bring up to the boil, then drop the temperature to the lowest point and simmer with the lid on for 10 minutes.

6. Turn off the heat, add the peas and quickly replace the lid to minimise the loss of heat. Set aside for a further 10-12 minutes with the lid securely on to finish the cooking process.

7. When ready to serve, stir through the chopped coriander and fork out into a bowl. Enjoy!

# GARLIC IN ASIAN CUISINE

Garlic is a key ingredient in most Asian cuisines, with the exception of Japanese. Although it does crop up in a few dishes, the Japanese, like the Brahmins, believe that garlic inflames the passions, so its use is very limited. This is certainly not so for the rest of Asia; in China, garlic, ginger and spring onion are the 'holy trinity' that forms the base of a huge number of dishes. A North Indian 'sofrito' would consist of garlic, ginger and onions, but garlic is also sliced and fried to give a different flavour and texture or employed as a garnish in the dish.

Green or immature garlic is also consumed widely in Asia. With a flavour similar to spring onion, it lacks the heat of mature garlic but brings flavour and aroma to the stir fries, soups and hotpots of Vietnam, Thailand, Myanmar, Laos, and China among others. Garlic leaves are popular too, often stir fried with eggs, meat or vegetables.

In Southern India garlic is treated almost as a vegetable, cooked slowly in a curry so that the cloves soften and sweeten, whereas in Burma it is used generously in pastes, sauces and garnishes. As far as Cambodia is concerned, it's probably easier to list the dishes that don't contain garlic! Modern Vietnamese cooks are using garlic in new ways: roasted garlic is served as a condiment, while garlic pastes and oils are now a feature of this cuisine. In Indonesia raw garlic is added to spicy sambals, stir fried with vegetables, cooked into curries or fried as a crispy garnish.

Garlic is considered to be an essential ingredient in Korean cuisine, and it appears in all manner of fish and meat dishes, while pickled garlic is enjoyed as a side dish and grilled garlic is paired with Korean barbecue. Thai people don't shy away from adding whole cloves of garlic to spicy salads and the cloves, skins and all, are fundamental to Thai curry pastes.

There may be different cooking techniques and degrees of pungency from country to country but there's no getting away from it: garlic is an integral part of the Asian diet. Being of Indian descent, I too am no stranger to a bulb of garlic. While I adore the cuisine of my heritage, in this book I have veered away from the traditional curries in favour of introducing some of the perhaps less familiar dishes of my youth, such as a fragrant Kashmiri garlicky cabbage stir fry.

As you can probably tell, I am a big fan of Asian food and have spread my culinary net far and wide to bring you some tantalising dishes from this region of the globe. You'll find a delicious slow roasted sweet vinegar and chicken dish from the Philippines, which is unctuous and utterly moreish. Then there's my take on a Malaysian style traybake: ridiculously easy, rich with the flavours of chicken satay, and beautiful to look at too. Veggies and carnivores alike will be knocked sideways by my recipe for Korean garlic and chilli tofu; it's a damascene conversion dish for tofu haters!

So, it's time to jump on board The Orient Express and find out for yourself what all the fuss is about. Enjoy the journey.

# COCONUT AND GARLIC TARKA DAAL

**PREPARATION TIME: 1 HOUR 20 MINUTES | COOKING TIME: 45 MINUTES | SERVES 4**

Warming, velvety and delicious, this recipe uses some of the most nutritious ingredients available at a super low cost; how could anything be more comforting? Tarka simply means an infusion where the whole spices, seeds and garlic are tempered in hot oil and then poured over the daal to add intense flavour that permeates throughout the whole dish. As a child I remember always wanting to be the first to have my serving so that I could take the deliciously crunchy garlic from the tarka on top, and I loved the gently garlic-infused oil too.

## INGREDIENTS

200g yellow moong daal

100g split channa daal

100ml hot water

2 x 400ml tins of creamed coconut milk

1 tsp turmeric

2 tsp salt, or to taste

2 tsp finely minced garlic

2 tsp finely minced fresh ginger

1 fresh green chilli, finely minced

1 tbsp finely chopped fresh coriander

**For the tarka**

2 tbsp oil

1 tsp black mustard seeds

1 tsp cumin seeds

½ tsp asafoetida

4 garlic cloves, finely sliced

1-2 whole green chillies, slit ¾ of the way up

Handful of fresh coriander leaves, to garnish

¼ red onion, finely diced

## METHOD

1.  Wash the lentils, then soak them for 1 hour in warm water. Rinse, drain and transfer to a large pan with the hot water and creamed coconut milk. Bring to the boil over a high heat, spooning off any frothy scum that rises to the surface. Once up to a rolling boil, reduce the heat and cook for 25-35 minutes, or until all the lentils are soft. You may need to top up the pan with hot water depending on the temperature and rate of the liquid evaporating.

2.  Once the lentils are cooked, add the turmeric, salt, garlic, ginger, green chilli, and fresh coriander. Mix well so that the spices are incorporated and cook for a further 5 minutes. Transfer to a serving bowl and keep warm.

3.  For the tarka, heat the oil in a separate deep pan. When the oil is hot, add the mustard seeds and wait for them to finish popping before adding the cumin seeds, asafoetida, sliced garlic and the whole green chillies. Keep the temperature low to ensure that the garlic infuses the oil and just starts to become golden and crispy.

4.  Remove from the heat and then pour the tarka over the cooked lentils. Garnish with the fresh coriander leaves and diced red onion, then enjoy this deliciously creamy tarka daal.

**Cook's Tip:** You could use just the moong daal on its own if you would prefer a smoother texture. Alternatively, you could add red lentils to this daal for a mixture of colours and textures.

# GARLIC, GINGER AND CHILLI CUCUMBERS

**PREPARATION TIME: 15 MINUTES | COOKING TIME: 40 MINUTES | SERVES 4**

Most people think cucumbers are a bit bland, boring and tasteless. I can understand why that might be, but they also have a great crunchy texture and are highly nutritious, packed with antioxidants that support brain health which is why they get my attention. In this recipe I've added my three musketeers: inflammation-fighting ginger which also helps with digestion, garlic for its mighty anti-microbial properties (great for gut health), and a delightfully umami chilli oil. The cucumber is also marinated in rice vinegar and soy sauce, then finished with toasted sesame seeds: a delicious side to enjoy with a burger or add to a salad.

## INGREDIENTS

400g baby cucumbers

½ tsp sugar

¾ tsp salt

2 tsp soy sauce

2 tsp rice vinegar

1 tbsp avocado oil

1 tbsp julienned fresh ginger

3 garlic cloves, finely chopped

Toasted sesame seeds and hot chilli oil, to serve

## METHOD

1. Start by quartering the baby cucumbers lengthways (if longer than 3 inches, halve them crosswise first) and placing them in a bowl. Add the sugar and salt, then let them stand for 30 minutes, tossing occasionally. Drain, then add the soy sauce and rice vinegar.

2. Heat the avocado oil in a small frying pan over a medium-high heat, add the ginger and garlic, and cook for about 30 seconds until fragrant.

3. Pour the garlic and ginger in the oil over the cucumbers and stir to combine all the ingredients. Season to taste and then transfer to a serving dish, discarding any liquid.

4. Sprinkle with toasted sesame seeds and finish with a drizzle of chilli oil.

# GARLICKY FRIED RICE

**PREPARATION TIME: 15 MINUTES | COOKING TIME: 15 MINUTES | SERVES 4**

There is always leftover rice in my house as food has to be elastic – you never know who's going to turn up for dinner at the last minute! – so I always make an extra portion. That said, nothing is ever wasted and my go-to with a little extra rice is to turn it into another meal that looks and tastes even better than the first, just like this aromatic delight. The trick to this dish is flavouring the oil with garlic first, and you also need to use rice that has been cooked and chilled at least the day before.

## INGREDIENTS

3 tbsp vegetable oil

8 garlic cloves, thinly sliced

2 banana shallots, finely diced

5cm fresh ginger, peeled and finely chopped

2 large eggs, beaten

500g pre-cooked and chilled basmati rice

1½ tsp salt

½ tsp black pepper

2 tsp toasted sesame oil

2 tsp toasted sesame seeds

2 tbsp finely chopped fresh coriander

4 spring onions, thinly sliced on the diagonal

1 lime, zested and juiced

## METHOD

1. Start by heating the oil in a large non-stick frying pan. Arrange the sliced garlic in a single layer and set over a low to medium heat. Cook, shaking the pan often, until the garlic is just golden and crisp – the oil should stop bubbling at this point, after about 4-5 minutes. Remove the garlic from the pan using a slotted spoon and transfer to a plate.

2. Using the same pan, increase the heat to medium and cook the shallots for 2-3 minutes until lightly golden, then add the ginger and stir well to combine. Cook for 2 minutes, stirring occasionally, until just softened and fragrant.

3. Now add the beaten eggs and stir rapidly to break up. Cook until just set, which will only take a few seconds.

4. Add the rice, salt, pepper, and sesame oil to the pan. Stir to combine and then leave it to cook undisturbed, pressing down with a spatula so the rice makes good contact with the pan until it begins to crisp up, which should take 2-3 minutes. Stir once, then press down again, cooking until you get more crispy bits.

5. Sprinkle over the toasted sesame seeds, fresh coriander, spring onions and lime zest, then add the lime juice and stir it all through the rice. Remove the pan from the heat.

6. Season the fried rice with salt and pepper to taste, then scatter the reserved garlic chips over the top and enjoy! If you want a little heat in the dish, sprinkle on a few chilli flakes too.

# MALAYSIAN FRAGRANT ROASTED CHICKEN

**PREPARATION TIME: 20 MINUTES, PLUS 1 HOUR MARINATING | COOKING TIME: 20 MINUTES | SERVES 4**

Malaysia is the spiritual home of fusion cuisine, drawing on influences from China, India, Indonesia, Portugal and even good old Great Britain! When the aromas from this fantastic dish start wafting through your kitchen, you'll be mentally transported to the street food markets of Penang and the lure of freshly cooked chicken satay, of which this recipe is so reminiscent. One word: enjoy.

## INGREDIENTS

4 tbsp soy sauce

4 tbsp sugar-free crunchy peanut butter

3 large banana shallots, finely chopped

2 red bullet chillies, thinly sliced

1 lime, zested and juiced

4 tsp finely minced garlic

2 tsp finely minced ginger

2 tsp dark brown sugar

1 tsp salt

½ tsp black pepper

2 tbsp freshly chopped coriander

1kg skinless chicken thigh fillets, each cut into 4 pieces

1 chicken stock cube

300ml chicken stock

## METHOD

1.  Preheat the oven to 200°c/180°c fan/gas mark 6.

2.  In a large mixing bowl, combine the soy sauce, peanut butter, shallots, chillies, lime zest and juice, garlic, ginger, sugar, salt, pepper, and 1 tablespoon of the chopped fresh coriander. Mix to a paste.

3.  Add the chicken to the bowl, massaging the paste into all the pieces to thoroughly coat them. Cover and set aside for 1 hour, time permitting.

4.  Lightly oil 2 baking trays with sides and lay the marinated chicken on them, leaving a gap between the pieces.

5.  Crumble the chicken stock cube and sprinkle it over the chicken. Place the tray in the preheated oven for 10 minutes, then pour in the chicken stock and turn the temperature down to 180°c/160°c fan/gas mark 4 for another 10 minutes or until cooked through.

6.  Pile the chicken into bowls along with any residual juices, then scatter the remaining fresh coriander over the top. Serve with steamed or coconut rice.

# KATCHU

PREPARATION TIME: 25 MINUTES, PLUS MARINATING OVERNIGHT | COOKING TIME: 25 MINUTES | SERVES 4

This dish was a spring classic in my childhood home, made at the first opportunity from young shoots of fresh green garlic. The vegetarian version I grew up with was a take on the meat version, made with raw ground lamb which was refrigerated overnight and 'cooked' by the heat of the raw garlic, ginger and lemon juice, almost like a marinade. This would be topped with sliced boiled eggs, garam masala and lots of freshly chopped coriander, then served almost like a main course pâté, drizzled with oil and enjoyed with plenty of fresh bread.

## INGREDIENTS

1kg Maris Piper potatoes

3 tbsp lemon juice

2 tbsp vegetable oil

1 tsp salt, or to taste

1 tsp ground turmeric

1 tsp garam masala, plus extra to garnish

2 tsp ground coriander

2 tsp ground roasted cumin

2 tsp finely chopped garlic

1 tsp finely chopped green chilli

6 tbsp finely chopped fresh coriander

50g green garlic stems, finely chopped

4 spring onions, finely chopped

4 fresh eggs

## METHOD

1.  Start by boiling the potatoes until tender, about 20 minutes. Drain the potatoes and allow them to cool a little before mashing.

2.  Put the mashed potato in a large bowl, then add the lemon juice, oil, salt and spices, garlic, chilli, half the fresh coriander, 40g of the green garlic, and the white parts of the spring onion (reserving the rest for garnish). Combine all the ingredients well.

3.  Transfer the mash to a serving dish that is suitable for the fridge and has about an inch of space left at the top for the eggs. Cover tightly and refrigerate overnight to allow the potato to absorb all the flavours.

4.  Remove the katchu from the fridge 1-2 hours before you want to serve. Hard boil the eggs, then peel and slice once they are cool enough.

5.  Lay the egg slices over the top of the katchu. Garnish with the remaining fresh coriander and green garlic, the reserved green spring onion, and a dusting of garam masala.

# MUSHROOMS WITH GARLIC AND CHILLI SAUCE

**PREPARATION TIME: 5 MINUTES | COOKING TIME: 5 MINUTES | SERVES 2 AS A SIDE**

This super simple recipe first made its debut in the original Cooking Academy dim sum class. To my surprise it quickly became the star of the show; no wonder really, as it's quick to prepare and cook yet is an absolute flavour bomb! Don't take my word for it, try it for yourself and see what you think.

## INGREDIENTS

2 tbsp soy sauce

2 tbsp finely chopped fresh coriander

3 tsp finely chopped garlic

2 heaped tsp jaggery

½ tsp ground black pepper, or chilli flakes to taste

20 chestnut mushrooms, halved or quartered depending on size

2 tbsp oil

2-3 tbsp sweet chilli sauce

Extra fresh coriander

## METHOD

1. Place the soy sauce, fresh coriander, garlic, jaggery, and pepper or chilli into a bowl and mix well, ensuring the jaggery has dissolved by rubbing it with your fingers.

2. Add the mushrooms to the bowl and gently massage the mixture into them. Set aside for 2-3 minutes.

3. Heat the oil in a large, shallow frying pan. Transfer the mushrooms from the bowl into the pan (reserving any remaining marinade) and cook on a medium-high heat for 3-4 minutes, turning the mushrooms to ensure they are coated and slightly crispy on all sides. If the pan isn't big enough to fit all the mushrooms in without crowding it, cook them in two batches.

4. Once the mushrooms are cooked, add the remaining marinade to one side of the pan and cook on a high heat to reduce.

5. Drizzle the sweet chill sauce over the mushrooms and cook for 30 seconds. Combine the mushrooms with the reduced marinade, stirring to coat them in the sauce.

6. Garnish with fresh coriander before serving.

# PAN SEARED SCALLOPS IN GARLIC AND COCONUT SAUCE

**PREPARATION TIME: 10 MINUTES | COOKING TIME: 8-10 MINUTES | SERVES 4**

Scallops are an expensive ingredient, so this is probably one for a special occasion – and special it will be! You'll get compliments galore for very little effort; the sweetness of the scallops is delightfully matched by the robust flavours in the dish, with the coconut milk adding a creamy sweetness which tempers the chilli heat. Sublime!

## INGREDIENTS

16 large sea scallops

2 tbsp oil for frying

Knob of butter

Salt and pepper

½ lime, cut into wedges

**For the sauce**

6 tbsp coconut milk

2 tbsp fish sauce

1 lime, juiced

2 tbsp chopped fresh coriander

3 tsp finely chopped garlic

½ tsp finely chopped fresh red chilli

½ tsp jaggery (natural unprocessed cane sugar)

## METHOD

1. Rinse the scallops and pat them dry. This is an important step to ensure they sear correctly.

2. Place a large frying pan over a medium heat, add the oil and butter, and when hot place the scallops into the pan, ensuring there is enough space in the pan to move them around freely. Cook without moving for 2 minutes (trying to turn them too early will cause the skin to tear). Season the scallops with salt and pepper while they cook.

3. After 2 minutes, gently turn the scallops over and season the other side. The scallops are ready when both sides have a crispy golden crust and are firm to the touch. Remove the scallops from the pan and place on absorbent kitchen paper to drain off any excess oil.

4. Now place all the ingredients for the sauce in the same pan used to cook the scallops on a medium-high heat. Stir gently from time to time. Cook for 2-3 minutes until the coriander and garlic become aromatic. Taste and season the sauce as needed; you could add more fish sauce, lime juice or sugar according to your preference.

5. Remove the pan from the heat, place the scallops on the serving plate, spoon the sauce over them and serve with a leaf salad. Garnish with the fresh lime wedges.

# PORK AND GARLIC MEATBALLS WITH NUOC CHAM DIPPING SAUCE (NEM NUONG)

**PREPARATION TIME: 10 MINUTES | COOKING TIME: 20 MINUTES | SERVES 4**

This super tasty recipe hails from Vietnam and the meatballs are extra special thanks to the inclusion of pork lardons. I serve a classic nuoc cham dipping sauce on the side which cuts through the richness of the pork while adding a citrus note and a kick of chilli.

## INGREDIENTS

### For the dipping sauce

25ml water

1 tsp rice vinegar

1 tsp sugar

¼ tsp finely chopped bird's eye chilli

1 tsp finely chopped garlic

1 tbsp fish sauce

½ lime, juiced (or 1 tbsp bottled lime juice)

### For the meatballs

½ tsp black pepper

1 tsp salt, or to taste

1 tsp sugar

½ tsp finely chopped bird's eye chilli

2 tsp fresh black peppercorns

3 tsp finely chopped garlic

1 tbsp fish sauce

2 tbsp finely chopped fresh coriander, or to taste

50g pork lardons (as fatty as possible – back fat would be used in Vietnam)

400g pork mince

## METHOD

1. First, make the dipping sauce. Bring the water to the boil along with the rice vinegar and sugar. Boil rapidly for 1 minute, then turn off the heat and allow to cool. Once cool, stir in the chilli, garlic, fish sauce and lime juice, then set aside.

2. Now prepare the meatballs. In a mixing bowl, combine the black pepper, salt, sugar, chilli, peppercorns, garlic, fish sauce and fresh coriander. Crush the peppercorns by pressing them against the side of the bowl using a wooden spoon.

3. Fry the lardons on a medium-high heat in a shallow frying pan for about 5-7 minutes until crisp. When they are ready, remove the lardons from the pan (save the frying pan to use later for the meatballs) and cut into very small cubes.

4. Add the lardons to the bowl and mix well, rubbing all the spices into them. Now add the minced pork and combine everything using one hand until well mixed.

5. Roll the pork mixture into balls about the size of walnuts. Reheat your frying pan and cook the meatballs for about 10 minutes. There is no need to add oil as the pork will render its fat once heated. Don't move the meatballs until the pork has cooked and bound together, otherwise they will fall apart. Once done, they should be golden brown all over.

6. When the meatballs are ready, they can be threaded onto wooden skewers if preferred, or just served in a bowl with the dipping sauce on the side.

# SLOW COOKED SWEET VINEGAR AND GARLIC CHICKEN

**PREPARATION TIME: 10 MINUTES, PLUS MARINATING | COOKING TIME: 1 HOUR 15 MINUTES | SERVES 4**

My Filipino-inspired slow cooked chicken comes from a friend and colleague who used to rave about the super-quick prep of this dish. The potent combination of vinegar, soy sauce, sugar and garlic acts as both a marinade and a beautiful silky sauce. Once the chicken is tender and the sauce reduces to a glossy consistency, it takes on a sweet and sour flavour that is delightful drizzled over a bowl of coconut rice and steamed baby bok choy.

## INGREDIENTS

120ml light soy sauce

120ml rice vinegar

120ml mirin

2 tbsp tamarind paste

2 tbsp jaggery (natural unprocessed cane sugar)

10 garlic cloves, peeled and lightly smashed

3 bay leaves

1 tsp black pepper

8 free-range chicken thighs, skin on and bone in

2 tbsp oil

## METHOD

1. In a large bowl or strong sealable bag, combine all the ingredients except the chicken and oil. Mix well, then add the chicken and rub the marinade into the meat, ensuring the marinade gets into all the crevices and the chicken is thoroughly coated. Cover the bowl or seal the bag and let it stand for at least 2 hours at room temperature or in the fridge overnight.

2. Remove the chicken from the marinade, reserving the liquid for later, and pat dry with paper towels.

3. Heat half the oil in a large sauté pan over a medium heat. Add half the chicken and cook until golden brown which should take approximately 4-5 minutes on each side. If this is happening too quickly, turn the heat down to a point where the chicken is getting sealed and crispy with a golden coating. Turn the pieces over and brown the other side in the same way, then transfer to a plate and repeat with the remaining oil and chicken.

4. Now return all the chicken and any juices to the pan along with the reserved marinade, making sure the liquid comes halfway up the sides of chicken (you may need to nestle them in). Bring to a simmer over a medium to high heat.

5. Once simmering, place the lid on the pan, lower the temperature to maintain a gentle simmer and cook for 50-60 minutes until the chicken is cooked through and tender.

6. When the chicken is cooked, discard the bay leaves, increase the heat to medium-high and reduce the liquid until syrupy.

7. Meanwhile, steam some whole baby bok choy for a few minutes to serve alongside the chicken with steamed or coconut rice. The flavour of this dish just gets better over time so be sure to make extra to have leftovers for lunch!

# SPICED CABBAGE STIR FRY

**PREPARATION TIME: 10 MINUTES | COOKING TIME: 15 MINUTES | SERVES 4**

Every recipe has a story of its own and this one is no exception. It dates back to my childhood when I hated anything with 'hot spices' in. I loved cabbage and garlic though, so I smothered my stir fry in creamy yoghurt to mask the heat. A few years later, I came to realise that spice wasn't so bad after all but still wanted to enjoy my cabbage the way I'd always had it. I often make this dish now because it's delicious and full of nostalgia. I also love that all the ingredients are so good for you!

## INGREDIENTS

500g savoy cabbage (or regular cabbage if you prefer)

3 tbsp vegetable oil

3 whole dried Kashmiri chillies

2 tsp black or brown mustard seeds

1 tsp English mustard

½ tsp asafoetida

½ tsp turmeric

6 large garlic cloves, thinly sliced

1 tsp salt

½ tsp black pepper

¼ chilli flakes (optional)

6 tbsp full-fat Greek yoghurt

1 tbsp finely chopped fresh coriander

## METHOD

1. Wash and drain the cabbage, then shake off the excess water and pat it dry. Cut or shred the cabbage thinly.

2. Heat the oil in a large frying pan (one with a lid) over a medium-high heat. Add the whole chillies and sauté for a few seconds before adding the mustard seeds. Allow them to finish popping and turn the heat down very low before adding the mustard, asafoetida, and turmeric.

3. Add the sliced garlic, stir to combine all the ingredients and cook on a low heat for 1 minute before adding the prepared cabbage. Increase the heat and stir to combine. You may need to add the cabbage in 2 or 3 stages to let it wilt before adding the next batch.

4. Now add the salt, pepper and chilli flakes, stir through and cook for 3-4 minutes with the lid on until the cabbage starts to wilt and reduces in the pan.

5. Add the yoghurt, stir through and then remove from the heat. Season to taste with more salt, pepper or chilli according to your preference.

6. Garnish the stir fry with fresh coriander, then serve immediately and enjoy.

# SPICY CRUNCHY GARLIC TOFU

**PREPARATION TIME: 1 HOUR 20 MINUTES | COOKING TIME: 10 MINUTES | SERVES 4**

If you're not a fan of tofu this recipe may be a bit of a game changer. The sauce is sticky, spicy and garlicky (of course). Pressing and frying the tofu gives it a really pleasing texture. We teach this dish in our Korean class and it's become a firm favourite with our students, tofu lovers and haters alike. Enjoy with an ice-cold beer, steamed rice and a generous drizzle of chilli sauce.

## INGREDIENTS

400g firm tofu, pressed and drained

3 tbsp + 2 tsp cornflour

1 tsp salt

3 tbsp honey

2 tbsp soy sauce

1½ tbsp gochujang

1 tbsp rice wine vinegar

1 tbsp mirin

4 tbsp vegetable oil

100g red onion, finely diced

4 tsp finely minced garlic

½ tsp fresh red chilli

3 spring onions, finely sliced Asian style

1 tbsp toasted sesame seeds

1 tbsp toasted sesame oil

## METHOD

1. Cut the prepared block of tofu into bite-size cubes. Mix the salt and 3 tablespoons of cornflour in a bowl, add the tofu and toss to coat. Set aside.

2. To make the sauce, combine the honey, soy sauce, gochujang, rice wine vinegar, and mirin with 2 teaspoons of cornflour in a small bowl. Set aside.

3. Heat half the vegetable oil in a large frying pan with deep sides. When the oil is hot, add the coated tofu pieces in one layer, making sure they are not touching each other. Cook the tofu pieces and flip them one by one until they are brown on all sides (approximately 7 minutes).

4. Remove the crispy tofu pieces from the pan and set them aside on kitchen paper to absorb any excess oil.

5. Using the same pan with the remaining oil, fry the red onion, garlic, chilli and spring onion (hold a few spring onions back for the garnish) until the garlic starts to brown.

6. Now add the sauce to the pan, stirring it until it thickens (approximately 30 seconds). Turn off the heat.

7. Add the fried tofu back to the pan and stir everything together, so that the tofu pieces are evenly coated in the sauce. Garnish with the sesame seeds, sesame oil and reserved spring onions. Serve with steamed rice or vegetables of your choice.

# THE ORIGINAL GARLIC INFUSED BOMBAY POTATOES

PREPARATION TIME: 10 MINUTES | COOKING TIME: 30 MINUTES | SERVES 4

Having previously showcased a wide range of Indian recipes in my first book, A Cupboard Full of Spices, I had resolved to veer away from Indian cuisine for the next outing. However, I have so many great garlic-centric recipes in my arsenal that I simply couldn't resist slipping a few in here and there. I urge you to try my recipe for Bombay potatoes without delay; it's a world away from the dish you would be served in a typical Indian restaurant.

## INGREDIENTS

500g baby new potatoes

2 tbsp rapeseed oil

1 tsp whole brown mustard seeds

1 tsp cumin seeds

12-15 fresh green garlic stalks, finely chopped (or spring onions if you can't get green garlic)

3 tsp finely chopped garlic

½ tsp chopped green chilli

½ tsp turmeric

¼ tsp asafoetida

¾ tsp salt, or to taste

¼ tsp ground black pepper

2 tbsp freshly chopped coriander

½ tsp kebab masala (or chaat masala if you can't get this)

## METHOD

1. First, boil the baby potatoes in salted water until just tender when pierced with a knife. Set aside and leave to cool.

2. Heat the oil in a wide pan and then add the mustard seeds. As they start to pop, turn the temperature down low while allowing enough heat to continue the popping process.

3. Once the seeds have finished popping, add the cumin seeds, green garlic, chopped garlic, green chilli, turmeric, asafoetida, salt, and black pepper.

4. Stir to combine everything, then immediately add the potatoes, turn up the heat and stir well to coat the potatoes with all the flavours. Cook for 4-5 minutes or until the potatoes are hot and slightly crispy.

5. Garnish your Bombay potatoes with the fresh coriander and a dusting of kebab masala.

**Cook's Tip:** You could add 300g of fresh baby spinach 2 minutes before taking the pan off the heat, moving it around the pan until the spinach has wilted evenly, for a fresh version of saag aloo. You could also stir some chopped spring onions (mainly the green parts) through the potatoes when the heat is turned off, which adds a slight crunch and gives the dish a nice finish.

# WILD GARLIC AND COURGETTE FRITTERS WITH GARLIC AND HERB YOGHURT

**PREPARATION TIME: 25 MINUTES | COOKING TIME: 15 MINUTES | MAKES ABOUT 12**

This is an alternative to my infamous onion bhaji recipe from my first book, A Cupboard Full of Spices. I like to shake it up a little with different vegetables and it's a great way to use the very underrated courgette. Squeezing the liquid out of the courgettes and using carbonated water are the secrets to crispy fritters. The garlic and herb dip is a regular go-to in my house, especially when we have fresh mint growing in the herb garden.

## INGREDIENTS

**For the garlic yoghurt**

150g natural yoghurt (not Greek)

3 garlic cloves, finely minced

2 tbsp finely chopped mint leaves

2 tbsp coarsely chopped coriander

2 tbsp lemon juice

1 tsp honey

¼ tsp salt and freshly ground pepper

1 tbsp extra virgin olive oil

**For the fritters**

250g courgettes

50g wild garlic leaves

1 small onion

130g gram flour

1 tbsp coriander seeds, smashed

1½ tsp Kashmiri chilli powder

1 tsp salt

1 tsp cumin seeds

1 tsp ground turmeric

½ tsp coarsely ground black pepper

1 tsp finely chopped ginger

3 tsp finely minced garlic

3 tbsp finely chopped fresh coriander (including tender stalks)

4 tbsp finely chopped mint leaves

Carbonated water, as needed

750ml vegetable oil

Sea salt

## METHOD

1. For the garlic yoghurt, mix everything except the oil together in a bowl and taste to check the seasoning. Cover and place in the fridge to chill. Dress with the oil when ready to serve.

2. For the fritters, grate the courgettes using the largest side of a box grater. Squeeze out as much water as possible and then place them in a sieve to drain further. Chop the wild garlic leaves and slice the onion very thinly, then set aside.

3. In a separate large mixing bowl, combine the gram flour, coriander seeds, chilli powder, salt, cumin, turmeric, black pepper, ginger, garlic, and fresh herbs (reserving a little of both for garnish later). Add a little carbonated water to the bowl and stir well to make a thick batter.

4. Squeeze any remaining water out of the grated courgette and start adding it to the batter along with the wild garlic and red onion. Hold back some of the vegetables to ensure you have the right proportion of batter, which should only be lightly coating all the vegetables. When it's the right consistency, you should be able to slide the mixture off your hand.

5. Heat the vegetable oil in a karahi or deep fryer over a medium-high heat. When the oil is hot but not smoking, work in batches to spoon scoops of mixture into the karahi or fryer, making little bird's nest shapes, no bigger than 1.5 inches in diameter. Cook the fritters until golden brown and crisp, then scoop them out of the pan and transfer to a bowl lined with absorbent paper towels to soak up any excess oil. Repeat with all the remaining batter.

6. Transfer the hot fritters to a serving dish. Sprinkle with sea salt and squeeze over a little fresh lemon juice. Top the bowl of garlic yoghurt with the reserved fresh mint and coriander, then serve with the delicious fritters.

# VIETNAMESE CARAMELISED FISH HOTPOT

**PREPARATION TIME: 10 MINUTES | COOKING TIME: 18 MINUTES | SERVES 4**

Caramel is Vietnam's signature flavour. It sounds unusual but once you add the fish sauce and lime, it transforms into something magical! Traditionally this dish would be cooked in a small clay pot, but you can use a heavy saucepan with a lid.

## INGREDIENTS

3 garlic cloves, finely sliced

3 tsp finely chopped garlic

2 tsp finely chopped ginger

½ tsp finely chopped bird's eye chilli

1 tbsp oil

1 tbsp jaggery

1 tbsp fish sauce

1 tbsp tamarind sauce

140ml coconut water or fish stock

4 pieces of salmon

### To serve

Chopped coriander or mint leaves

Steamed rice

Green vegetables (such as bok choy)

Lime wedges

## METHOD

1. In a small bowl, mix all the garlic, ginger and chilli together.

2. Heat the oil in a medium saucepan, add the garlic mixture and cook over a medium heat until softened.

3. Mix the jaggery with a tablespoon of water, then add it to the saucepan. Heat for about 2-3 minutes until the sugar is melted, bubbling and slightly sticky.

4. Add the fish sauce, tamarind, and coconut water or fish stock. Stir well and bring the broth to a simmer.

5. Now add the salmon fillets to the broth. Place the lid on and let them simmer for 5-8 minutes or until the fish is cooked through (thicker fillets might take another minute or two).

6. Add some fresh coriander or mint to the hotpot and serve with steamed rice, green vegetables, and lime wedges.

# THAI CARAMELISED CHICKEN (KAI YAANG)

PREPARATION TIME: 20 MINUTES | COOKING TIME: 10 MINUTES | SERVES 4 AS A SNACK OR STARTER

This recipe really is a doddle to make, yet it hits all the right notes in the Thai flavour pantheon. It's absolutely delicious when served in a little gem lettuce leaf, as the cool crispness contrasts beautifully with the intensely flavoured chicken. It makes a great starter for sharing or a light lunch. Be sure to squeeze a little fresh lime over the top with a drizzle of sriracha sauce to make the flavours really pop.

## INGREDIENTS

2 lemongrass stalks, outer casing removed and finely sliced (use previously frozen lemongrass if possible, as it will be easier to blend)

2 tsp crushed fresh peppercorns

5 garlic cloves, peeled

1 tbsp jaggery

½ tsp salt

2½ tbsp oil

1 tbsp fish sauce

3 tbsp finely chopped coriander (use as much stalk as possible for flavour)

400g chicken thighs, cut into 3 or 4 pieces depending on the size

Fresh lime wedges and sriracha sauce, to serve

## METHOD

1. Place the lemongrass, fresh peppercorns, garlic, jaggery, salt, and 2 tablespoons of the oil into a food processor. Blitz to a rough paste, scraping down as you go and making sure you have broken down as much of the fibrous lemongrass as possible.

2. Now add the fish sauce and fresh coriander, then continue blitzing to a smooth creamy paste. Remove this from the food processor and transfer to a mixing bowl.

3. Add the chicken pieces to the bowl and massage the paste into the chicken very thoroughly until completely coated. Cover the bowl and set aside at room temperature for at least an hour, time permitting, or in the fridge if you can leave it to marinate for longer.

4. When you're ready to cook the chicken, heat a heavy-based frying pan or cast iron grill pan, add the remaining oil and place the marinated chicken pieces in the pan. Be careful not to overcrowd the pan and cook the chicken in batches if necessary. Cook the chicken on a very low heat, allowing it to caramelise but remain tender, for about 5 minutes on each side or until cooked through and the juices run clear when the chicken is pierced with a knife.

5. Finish the chicken with a squeeze of fresh lime juice and a drizzle of sriracha sauce.

# GARLIC IN SAUCES AND CONDIMENTS

*"Condiments are like old friends – highly thought of, but often taken for granted." – Marilyn Kaytor*

The first known condiment was of course salt, swiftly followed by its partner in crime, vinegar. It's not certain when the first recipe for aioli originated, but it's likely that it emerged from the ancient Egyptian and Mediterranean civilisations and could well be the first known inclusion of garlic in a sauce. Garlic really started to make its presence felt in the Indian chutneys of the 17th century, then 1835 brought the advent of Worcestershire Sauce which featured garlic as a main player. Nowadays, it's a staple ingredient in everything from mayonnaise to sriracha sauce.

Condiments are the unsung heroes of the dining table, frequently coming to the rescue by elevating a bland or uninteresting dish. There are the usual suspects of course: ketchup, brown sauce, mayo et al, which we often reach for unthinkingly and which frankly often mask the true flavour of a dish. But there's also a whole host of exciting accompaniments out there that serve to enhance a dish rather than overwhelm it.

Don't get me wrong, I'm certainly no stranger to a shop-bought sauce; in fact, I find that both tomato ketchup and brown sauce are great flavour enhancers when dolloped into a stew or bolognaise. However, a homemade condiment ticks a lot of boxes. Take my recipe for garlic confit for example: make a vinaigrette with a few of the cloves, smash and stir them through any vegetable dish, top a pizza with both the confit cloves and a drizzle of garlicky oil… the possibilities are endless.

If you want to jazz up a plain piece of meat or fish, a compound butter is another quick and easy seasoning solution; there are three ideas in this chapter to get you started but the only limit is your imagination… a little bit of leftover harissa sauce, for example, would be fabulous incorporated into a butter. My homemade garlic pesto is a winner too; just toss some cooked pasta through it for a quick, delicious and satisfying meal.

If you're after something a little bit different to ring the changes, may I recommend the zaalouk dip on the next page? Or how about a flavoured oil? I've got a great chilli and garlic oil which is simply sensational on eggs, among many other things. If heat's not your thing, try making my garlic and parsley oil: it won't disappoint!

In short, you can effortlessly make every meal a celebration by stocking your fridge with a selection of homemade goodies. Trust me, you'll be glad you did!

# INTENSELY DELICIOUS ZAALOUK DIP

**PREPARATION TIME: 10-15 MINUTES | COOKING TIME: 50-55 MINUTES | SERVES 4**

I think aubergines are highly underrated and this is possibly a throw back to when vegetables were simply boiled to death if you didn't know what to do with them. Thankfully, we've come a long way since then and when simple vegetables are paired with herbs and spices, they become delicious in every way, not to mention highly nutritious. I often use them as a spread on flatbreads, as with this recipe. I prefer my zaalouk served lukewarm on hot flatbread or toasted sourdough bread.

## INGREDIENTS

2 large aubergines

4 tbsp olive oil, plus extra for drizzling

4 garlic cloves, finely chopped

5 very ripe tomatoes, finely chopped (300g)

2 tbsp tomato purée

2 bay leaves

2 tsp ground cumin

1 tsp paprika

¼ tsp dried chilli flakes (optional)

1 tsp jaggery or brown sugar

½ tsp salt

½ tsp coarsely ground black pepper

120ml vegetable stock

1 tbsp pomegranate molasses

¼ of a lemon, juiced

Small handful of coriander, finely chopped

## METHOD

1.  Preheat the oven to 180°c/160°c fan/gas mark 4. Wash and dry the aubergines, then prick them all over with a skewer and rub with oil. Place on a tray and roast in the oven for 45-50 minutes or until tender inside and crispy on the outside. You should be able to poke a skewer into the charred skin straight through to the flesh when it's cooked. Once cool, remove and discard the skin. Cut off the tops and finely chop the flesh. Set aside.

2.  Meanwhile, heat 3 tablespoons of the oil in a pan over a medium heat, add the garlic and cook for 10 seconds until fragrant. Add the chopped tomatoes, tomato purée and bay leaves, stir well, and cook with the lid on for 8-9 minutes before adding the cumin, paprika, chilli flakes, sugar, salt and pepper.

3.  Cook for 3-4 minutes until the spices have infused the tomatoes and the mixture resembles a roux. Add the stock, mix well and bring to the boil. Cover, reduce the heat and simmer for 8-10 minutes, stirring occasionally, or until the tomatoes have broken down.

4.  Now add the aubergine to the sauce along with the pomegranate molasses. Stir well, season to taste and cook for a further 5 minutes, stirring occasionally, or until the sauce is deliciously thick. Add the lemon juice and coriander, folding them through the sauce.

5.  Give the zaalouk a final drizzle of olive oil and then serve immediately with pitta or flatbread. Enjoy with deep satisfaction!

# GARLIC CONFIT

**PREPARATION TIME: 30-40 MINUTES | COOKING TIME: 60-90 MINUTES | MAKES 2 SMALL JAM JARS**

My garlic confit is a Big Little Recipe with the smallest possible ingredient list but loads of everything else: flavour, creativity, wow factor!

Since I'm not so big on meats I make many other types of confit such as onion, mushroom, and aubergine, to name just a few. But I think my garlic confit is standout and a go-to condiment for upgrading just about anything, from carrot soup to avocado toast or even simple steamed broccoli. Peeling the garlic is the hardest part of this recipe, and it goes a lot faster if you have a podcast or audiobook playing in the background. From there, it's entirely hands off, simmering away, while you kick back and enjoy your favourite tipple.

The cooking time will vary according to your stove, but the most important thing is that it should be done as slowly as possible. Check in every so often to make sure the garlic is bubbling gently, not vigorously. A little patience will yield buttery soft cloves and deeply flavoured oil. Speaking of which, I recommend olive oil here because the beautiful fruity flavour and grassiness works so well with garlic. But if you want your confit oil to have a subtler flavour, just swap in the same quantity of rapeseed or vegetable oil.

## INGREDIENTS

5 large garlic bulbs (325g peeled weight)

400ml olive oil

## METHOD

1. Break the garlic bulbs into cloves, peel off all the skins and trim the ends. Combine the garlic cloves and olive oil in a small saucepan over a low heat and bring to a gentle simmer.

2. Lower the heat as much as possible to maintain a gentle simmer for 1 to 1½ hours, until the cloves are very tender and golden brown.

3. Transfer the confit to a sterilised airtight glass jar, making sure the cloves are submerged in the oil, and refrigerate for up to 2 weeks. You can also freeze the confit in an airtight container for up to 3 months.

**Cook's Tip:** Spread the confit cloves on grilled bread, marinate olives and feta with the garlicky oil, mash cloves into store-bought mayo or stir into mashed potatoes.

**Note:** Garlic bulbs can vary enormously in size, so in my recipes an average garlic bulb has around 12 cloves and weighs around 65g when peeled.

# CHIMICHURRI SAUCE

**PREPARATION TIME: 10 MINUTES | SERVES 4**

My mission in life is to make cooking more appealing and compelling for my audience. I want everyone to cook fresh meals to nourish themselves and feel the benefits, so I'm always looking for ways in which I can turn a simple ingredient into something delicious and nutritious in little or no time. This means having a well-stocked fridge with all kinds of sauces you can pull out to pair up with others and turn lunch or dinner into something celebratory on each occasion, rather than feeling you have to go to a restaurant to do that.

My chimichurri is a bright and vibrant pesto-like sauce containing herbs, garlic and tangy vinegar that can be used with chicken, chops, steaks, vegetables, grains, and salad. It lasts for two to three weeks in the fridge so you can make plenty and have quick solutions for meals at whatever time of day, even breakfast. If you can, make the chimichurri a day before serving to give the flavours time to meld.

The nutritional profile of this sauce is huge with every ingredient; the fresh coriander is rich in antioxidants that provide immune-boosting properties, while the garlic is supreme for digestion and gut health, helping up build up your good bacteria. Parsley is full of vitamin C and iron, and chilli helps to keep you regular and speed up your metabolism.

## INGREDIENTS

50g fresh flat leaf parsley leaves

50g fresh coriander leaves and tender stalks

5g fresh oregano leaves (or 2 tsp dried oregano)

5 fat garlic cloves, peeled and smashed

2 spring onions, trimmed

1 tsp chilli flakes

½ tsp salt

½ tsp ground black pepper

60ml red wine vinegar

300ml extra virgin olive oil

## METHOD

1. Place all the ingredients except the oil into a food processor. Process until finely chopped, stopping and scraping down the sides of the bowl with a rubber spatula as needed. This should only take about a minute in total.

2. With the motor running, add the oil to the processor in a steady stream. Scrape down the sides of the bowl and pulse a few times to combine until you are happy with the consistency.

3. Transfer the sauce to an airtight container and refrigerate for at least 2 hours or up to 1 day to allow the flavours to meld. Before serving, stir and season as needed.

4. Sit back and look forward to easy midweek meals!

# A VERY TASTY TOMATO CHUTNEY

**PREPARATION TIME: 10 MINUTES | COOKING TIME: 40 MINUTES | MAKES 1 X 250G JAR**

I have a small fridge to store all my condiments, sauces and pickles in – almost like a larder cupboard – because they form part of my weekly repertoire, trusted friends I can turn to for any meal. I don't always have time to cook and versatile chutneys such as this one can be paired with breads or eggs to make a simple supper or a quick sandwich for lunch that never needs to be boring. I also use this as a chutney for my cheeseboard which is a weekly treat!

## INGREDIENTS

2 tsp cumin seeds

2 tbsp olive oil

1 banana shallot, finely diced (50g)

2 fresh red bullet chillies, finely chopped (use a hotter variety if you prefer)

6 fat garlic cloves, finely minced

2 tsp finely grated ginger

2 tsp smoked paprika

1 tsp fennel seeds

1 tsp salt

600g tinned plum tomatoes

100g jaggery or soft brown sugar

50ml red wine vinegar

## METHOD

1. In a large frying pan, toast the cumin seeds over a low to medium heat until they are just aromatic. Transfer to a pestle and mortar and grind to a powder.

2. Gently heat the olive oil in the same saucepan, add the shallot and cook for 7-8 minutes on a low heat before adding the chilli, garlic and ginger. Cook gently for a further 2-3 minutes until beautifully aromatic and softened.

3. Add the ground cumin, smoked paprika, fennel seeds, and salt to the pan. Stir to combine and cook for 1 minute before adding the tomatoes. Turn up the heat to medium to bring the mixture to a simmer and use the back of a wooden spoon to break up the tomatoes.

4. Add the sugar and vinegar. Cook without the lid for 20-25 minutes or until the chutney becomes thick and glossy. Remove from the heat and leave to cool before storing. This will keep in a jar in the fridge for up to 3 months.

# AIOLI

PREPARATION TIME: 10 MINUTES | MAKES 200G

The famous French garlic mayonnaise, which originated in Provence. It's simply garlic a-go-go, with a hint of tarragon for a subtle liquorice hit.

## INGREDIENTS

3 large garlic cloves, minced

2 large egg yolks

225ml extra virgin olive oil

1 tbsp lemon juice

1 tbsp lime juice

1 tbsp Dijon mustard

1 tbsp chopped tarragon

Salt and pepper, to taste

## METHOD

1. Ensure that all the ingredients are at room temperature. Blend the garlic and egg yolks in a food processor until combined.

2. With the motor running, add the oil drop by drop until the mixture starts to thicken. Now add the oil in a slow, steady stream until the mixture has thickened to the consistency of mayonnaise.

3. Add the lemon and lime juice, mustard, and tarragon to the processor, then blend until smooth. Season to taste with salt and pepper.

4. Store any leftovers in the fridge – it will keep for up to 1 week in an airtight container.

# SMOKED GARLIC HUMMUS DRESSING

PREPARATION TIME: 10 MINUTES | MAKES 280G

Whoever thought of combining hummus – the food of the gods – with smoky, sweet garlic deserves a medal. Oh, hang on a minute: that would be me! Drizzle this over salad, grilled meats, pan-fried halloumi… the possibilities are endless. Just three little words: this is yummy.

## INGREDIENTS

400g tinned chickpeas, drained

40ml lemon juice

20ml water

2 tbsp tahini

2 tbsp olive oil

4 tsp Bart's smoked garlic paste

½ tsp sea salt

Pinch of ground black pepper

2 tbsp pine nuts, toasted

## METHOD

1. Put all the ingredients except the pine nuts into a food processor and blitz until smooth. Add a little more water if necessary to get the right consistency.

2. Drizzle the dressing over anything you like and sprinkle with the toasted pine nuts.

# CREAMY GARLIC AND PORCINI MUSHROOM SAUCE/SALAD DRESSING

**PREPARATION TIME: 5 MINUTES | COOKING TIME: 5 MINUTES | MAKES 200ML**

If anchovy is hailed as the bacon of the sea, I would say that mushrooms are the bacon of the vegetable kingdom. They are full of flavour and can imbue so many dishes with subtle savoury depth, much like other umami ingredients. Forget the slimy or watery versions you may have encountered before; mushrooms can be transformational when cooked properly.

In this recipe, porcini mushroom paste is paired with cream and black garlic to create a sauce that's great as a base for pasta dishes, but also works brilliantly as a salad dressing for the more robust, bitter leaves such as cos lettuce, red radicchio or chicory. It's delicious lavished on fried or toasted bread for a crostini or crouton too. I always make this ahead of time as I find that the flavour mellows, but it must be served at room temperature for the right texture, which creates a beautiful mouthfeel. Finally, I would finish the dish with some crushed walnuts on top. Voilà!

## INGREDIENTS

180ml double cream

2 tsp black garlic paste

3 tsp porcini mushroom paste

2 good pinches of ground nutmeg

¼ tsp sweet paprika

Pinch of black pepper

Extra virgin olive oil, to drizzle

1-2 drops of white wine vinegar, to taste

## METHOD

1.  Gently heat the double cream in a small saucepan. Add the black garlic paste, mushroom paste, nutmeg, paprika, and black pepper, stirring gently to combine.

2.  Simmer until the mushroom and garlic pastes have dissolved into the cream and the sauce has thickened a little. Remove from the heat and cover with a lid or a plate, leaving it to cool.

3.  When you're ready to serve, whisk the sauce vigorously until it loosens and smooths out. Drizzle in a little extra virgin olive oil and a few drops of good vinegar, then it's ready to enjoy.

**Cook's Tip:** If you are using this recipe for mushroom crostini, I would recommend stir-frying your chosen mushrooms separately before folding the sauce through them and serving on the crostini.

# GARLIC CHILLI OIL

**PREPARATION TIME: 10 MINUTES | MAKES 120ML**

This quick and easy garlic chilli oil is made in minutes with a few simple ingredients. It's perfect for drizzling over ramen noodle bowls, sautéing veggies, dunking dumplings and potstickers, and so much more!

## INGREDIENTS

120ml vegetable oil

3 garlic cloves, finely chopped

1 tbsp toasted sesame seeds

1 tbsp crushed red chilli flakes

## METHOD

1. Put the crushed red chilli flakes in a small heatproof bowl and set aside.

2. Heat the oil in a saucepan over a medium heat. Add the garlic and stir frequently until just beginning to turn golden, approximately 2 minutes.

3. Stir in the sesame seeds and cook for another minute until the garlic is crisp and golden. Take care not to overcook the garlic as it will continue cooking in the oil even when off the heat.

4. Carefully pour the garlic and sesame oil into the bowl of chilli flakes. Mix well and allow to cool before storing in a sterilised bottle.

# THE ULTIMATE GARLIC MARINADE FOR STEAK

**PREPARATION TIME: 5 MINUTES | MAKES ENOUGH FOR 6 STEAKS**

The marination of meat can be traced back to the Renaissance when it was used to preserve and season food. Nowadays we're looking for marinades to inject great flavour and improve texture. My marinade for steak is as good as it gets: sweet, salty, sticky and rich, it will take any meat to the next level. Don't just restrict it to steak; try it with lamb, chicken and pork too. The balsamic vinegar will help to tenderise the meat while the soy sauce and honey will work with the natural sugars in the protein for optimum caramelisation and depth of flavour.

## INGREDIENTS

3 tbsp balsamic vinegar

3 tbsp dark soy sauce

2 tbsp honey

2 tbsp finely minced garlic

1 tbsp Worcestershire sauce

1 tsp ground black pepper

1 tsp onion powder

½ tsp flaky sea salt

## METHOD

1. Mix all the ingredients together and pour into a resealable plastic bag. Add your steak (or other meat) and marinate for a minimum of 2 hours before cooking. That's it! Enjoy.

# SLOW ROASTED ONION AND GARLIC DIP THAT GOES WITH EVERYTHING

**PREPARATION TIME: 10 MINUTES | COOKING TIME: 50 MINUTES | MAKES 300G**

It does what it says on the tin… I hope you grow to love this gorgeous little dip as much as I do. It also makes the house smell just amazing, and people think you're a wonderful cook! I use leftover tortilla wraps or any breads to make large croutons for dipping into and eating this. Just one word of caution, you might smell of onion bagels afterwards!

## INGREDIENTS

200g red onions, peeled and thinly sliced

100g white onions, peeled and thinly sliced

2 garlic bulbs

80ml olive oil

30ml water

1 tsp salt

5 tbsp full-fat Greek yoghurt

1 tbsp lemon juice

½ a lemon, zested

1 tsp black pepper

½ tsp sea salt

Chilli flakes and chopped parsley, to garnish (optional)

## METHOD

1. Preheat the oven to 170°c/150°c fan/gas mark 3. Place the sliced onions on a large baking sheet lined with parchment paper. Lightly press down on the garlic cloves to open them a little but ensure they remain within the skin, then add them to the onions on the tray. Add the oil, water and salt, then toss together until thoroughly combined. Place the tray in the preheated oven and cook for 30-35 minutes until caramelised (they should not be charred).

2. Remove the tray from the oven and transfer the onions to a chopping board. When cool enough to handle, chop the onions very finely. Remove the soft garlic from the skins using the blade of your knife to squash the cloves and make a coarse purée.

3. Put the garlic and chopped onions into a food processor and blitz until they are combined into a smooth purée. Transfer this to a bowl, add the yoghurt, lemon juice and zest, black pepper, and sea salt, then stir well to combine.

4. Taste the dip to check the seasoning and adjust as needed. If you like, garnish with chilli flakes and a sprinkle of fresh parsley to serve.

# TURKISH CHILLI SAUCE

**PREPARATION TIME: 10 MINUTES | COOKING TIME: 20 MINUTES | MAKES 500ML**

This simple little sauce is a great accompaniment to the chicken shish kebabs on page 96 but is also delicious served with warm flatbreads. There's just a hint of heat from the chilli, layered under the sweet and savoury notes, and its depth of flavour belies the simplicity of its execution. Try it on eggs too and brighten up a midweek breakfast.

## INGREDIENTS

1 red onion, roughly chopped

2 shallots, roughly chopped

1 fat red chilli, roughly chopped (leave the seeds in)

3 tbsp olive oil

3 tsp finely minced garlic

2 tbsp sun-dried tomato purée

2 tbsp dark brown sugar

400g tinned chopped tomatoes

2 tsp lemon juice

½ tsp black pepper

½ tsp salt

## METHOD

1. Put the red onion, shallot and chilli into a food processor and blitz to a smooth paste.

2. Heat the oil gently in a frying pan and fry the onion paste with the minced garlic and tomato purée for 5 minutes.

3. Now add the brown sugar, tinned tomatoes, lemon juice, black pepper, and salt to the pan. Bring to the boil and then simmer for 25 minutes.

4. Take off the heat and leave to cool before storing. For a smoother sauce, blitz the ingredients with a hand blender. The sauce will keep in the fridge for 5 days and can also be frozen.

# GARLIC PARSLEY OIL

**PREPARATION TIME: 5 MINUTES | MAKES 200ML**

As you probably know by now, my fridge is always full of immensely useful things designed to make cooking a pleasurable experience rather than a chore. The way to do this is having lots of tricks up your sleeve so that when time is very tight, you can still eat like a queen and feel you have nourished yourself as you should.

Arguably you could call this a pesto though it doesn't include parmesan or nuts, so the consistency is somewhat thinner, but is still just as delicious and useful. I use this whenever I want to add a bit of depth to a dish and frequently drizzle it over garlic bread, eggs, pasta, or salad as a rich dressing.

It's made in minutes and provides wonderful nutrition and flavour for weeks afterwards. This recipe will make about 200ml (and that's never enough!). When sitting in the fridge it may congeal so I would recommend taking it out of the fridge well before use and leaving it in a warm kitchen.

## INGREDIENTS

70g garlic cloves, peeled

25g parsley leaves, roughly chopped

200ml extra virgin olive oil

4 tsp lemon juice

½ tsp black pepper

¼ tsp salt

## METHOD

1. Place the ingredients into a blender and process until smooth. This will keep in a sterilised airtight jar in the fridge for up to 1 month.

# A TRIO OF GARLIC BUTTERS

**PREPARATION TIME: 15 MINUTES EACH | MAKES 9 TABLESPOONS EACH**

Fragrant garlic butters are easy to make and very versatile; they can add masses of flavour to meats, prawns, potatoes, and toasted breads. The three recipes here couldn't be any easier: simply add garlic to good quality butter and then season with sea salt, black pepper, and whatever aromatics you like. Since it freezes and refrigerates wonderfully, you'll be able to use a tablespoon or two whenever you want to add a bit of garlicky goodness to your recipes! I add mine to jacket potatoes, grilled asparagus with a fried egg or two, hot flatbreads… the options really are endless.

## INGREDIENTS

### For the Roasted Garlic Butter

2 garlic bulbs

2 tsp olive oil

1 tsp sea salt

1 tsp coarsely ground black pepper

120g unsalted butter, at room temperature

### For the Chilli and Lemon Garlic Butter

8 garlic cloves, peeled

1 bullet chilli, finely chopped

1½ lemons, zested

2 tsp olive oil

1 tsp sea salt

1 tsp coarsely ground black pepper

120g unsalted butter, at room temperature

### For the Green Garlic and Herb Butter

8 garlic cloves, peeled

15 strands of green garlic (or chives)

10 sprigs of parsley, leaves only

1 tsp fresh or dried oregano

2 tsp olive oil

1 tsp sea salt

1 tsp coarsely ground black pepper

120g unsalted butter, at room temperature

## METHOD

### For the Roasted Garlic Butter

1. Preheat the oven to 180°c/160°c fan/gas mark 4. Cut about a third off the top of each garlic bulb, leaving the cloves exposed. Peel off some of the papery outer skin.

2. Place the bulbs on a sheet of foil, drizzle with the olive oil, season with the salt and pepper, then wrap in the foil and place on a baking tray.

3. Roast the garlic for about 30 minutes or until soft, then remove from the oven and leave to cool completely. Once cooled, squeeze all the soft garlic out of the skins.

4. In a food processor, combine the roasted garlic with the butter and pulse several times until smooth. Scoop out, wrap in clingfilm and roll into a sausage. Place in the fridge to chill.

### For the Chilli and Lemon Garlic Butter

1. In a food processor, combine all the ingredients and pulse several times until smooth.

2. Scoop out the butter, wrap it in clingfilm and roll into a sausage. Place in the fridge to chill.

### For the Green Garlic and Herb Butter

1. In a food processor, combine all the ingredients and pulse several times until smooth.

2. Scoop out the butter, wrap it in clingfilm and roll into a sausage. Place in the fridge to chill.

**Cook's Tip:** Store the garlic butter in your fridge in a sealed container or resealable plastic bag. Use within 3 weeks. Alternatively, cut the chilled roll of butter into discs and freeze in a resealable bag.

# WILD GREEN GARLIC PESTO

**PREPARATION TIME: 10 MINUTES | MAKES 1-2 JAM JARS**

This recipe is a garlic lover's dream and, for me, a beautiful moment of nostalgia going back to my childhood, tending to the herb garden in my family home. I've grown up with green garlic, eaten it in all its stages, and have yet to find a green garlic recipe that doesn't please my palate. I love this pesto dolloped over a fried egg: one of my many guilty pleasures. Hard neck garlic plants are essentially garlic bulbs that are pulled out of the ground before they dry, when the skin becomes papery. You will most likely find them in speciality markets or Asian fresh produce markets. If you can't get hard neck garlic, just use the usual garlic bulbs, though you will need less as the flavour of garlic develops as the bulb dries. Equally, if you don't manage to forage for wild garlic you can easily replace it with spinach, chives and extra garlic cloves.

## INGREDIENTS

200g young heirloom wild hard necked green garlic plants

200g freshly grated parmesan

150g hazelnuts

100g wild garlic leaves

8 tbsp extra virgin olive oil

2 tbsp white wine

1 lemon, juiced

1 tsp salt

½ tsp black pepper

## METHOD

1. Prepare your green garlic plants by topping and tailing them. Discard the roots so you are left with the premature bulbs and tender green leaves. Wash the leaves and pat dry.

2. Put all the ingredients into a food processor and blend on a high speed until you achieve a uniform texture. Taste and season as required before removing from the food processor. Add more cheese for more creaminess or umami flavour. Add more wine or lemon juice for more acidity or to make it more piquant. Add more olive oil for a smoother blend.

3. Serve the pesto with anything you like – it's great with pasta, roasted vegetables, flatbreads… in my humble opinion there's no wrong way to eat green garlic pesto!

# ACKNOWLEDGEMENTS

Writing is often considered a solitary occupation and yet the making of a cookbook is far from solitary, rather a collaboration of a great team of people who have been involved in some way or another to take an idea or dream and make it a reality, so I have many people to thank.

My team and colleagues here at The Cooking Academy are amazing and I particularly want to thank them for their support, encouragement, two penneth of advice, and random ideas that are always welcome. Gosia, you always get behind a project – and I thank you for your grounding – you are a stalwart. Paul Gregory, who was responsible for not just the beautiful photography of the book but so much of the food styling, a role he absorbed without rancour. I am sure I tested his patience no end. Thanks to Katie, my editor at Meze Publishing, and of course Paul Cocker for his creative input in the layout and design.

Inspiration comes from many sources and so I would also like to thank the authors of the books I have read and cooked from that have inspired me over the last 20 years in my food journey. Academic research is vital for a book of this nature and my particular thanks go to the American Journal of Clinical Nutrition, National Institutes of Health, European Journal of Molecular and Clinical Medicine, Cambridge University, and the many researchers who have been able to demonstrate the efficacy of garlic in clinical trials all over the world.

But most of all, I am, as ever, indebted to Sarah Leary who I thank wholeheartedly for holding my hand and my pen throughout my writing journey and dream of becoming a published author. The Garlic Story would not have been possible without her. She has been instrumental in enabling this book and has meticulously steered me through every page and stage. My sister from another mister – I thank you always from the bottom of my heart.

# ABOUT THE AUTHOR

Kumud Gandhi is a food writer, critic and author, broadcaster, food scientist, and professional speaker. She is also the founder of an award-winning cookery school, The Cooking Academy, based in Hertfordshire in the UK. In 2018 she wrote her best-selling cookery book, A Cupboard Full of Spices, and has been named 'The Spice Queen' by BBC food journalist Nick Coffer.

Kumud was born and raised in England, the daughter of Indian parents who emigrated in the 1950s, and attributes her scientific approach to food to the three generations of chemists and spice merchants in her family. As a child she travelled extensively throughout Southeast Asia and spent time with her aunts and great aunts learning about the many herbs, spices and vegetables that were a feature of their day-to-day life, forming the foundations of what was to become her life's work.

After graduating from the London School of Economics, Kumud moved into the world of corporate banking and finance which brought further opportunities to travel and enhance her knowledge of gastronomy, particularly throughout Asia and the Middle East. While taking a career break, Kumud made the decision to follow her true passion by retraining in food and nutrition at The London Food Centre. In 2007, she founded The Saffron House fine dining company and catered for many prestigious clients including Nelson Mandela and King Charles III.

Kumud founded The Cooking Academy in 2010, a cookery school based in Rickmansworth borne out of her passion for nutritional and medicinal health using food as a tool for overall wellness. The cookery school takes a unique approach to sharing this subject with its students, putting the beneficial properties of ingredients at the heart of everything. Combining the science of food and nutrition with great taste in wholesome yet delicious recipes, The Cooking Academy aims to enable anyone – including the children and young adults it works with through the Duke of Edinburgh Awards – to take their culinary skills to the next level.

Kumud loves to educate others about her specialist subjects, which include gut health and managing the symptoms of menopause through diet. As a renowned public speaker on 'The Alchemy of Food' and 'Eating for Immunity & Gut Health', Kumud explores why we eat what we eat, how food has evolved and what has influenced our food habits over the millennia. She is also a regular contributor to the BBC as a food expert, including BBC 1's Rip Off Britain and BBC Radio 4's Today Programme, as well as writing for The Times, The Telegraph, and Health Magazine among other publications.

Since forging her new career in food, Kumud has returned to the corporate world – this time sharing her passion and philosophy on health and wellbeing for people in the workplace. She has been a keynote speaker at numerous high-profile events and conferences including the IOD and Oxford University, advocating for 'Wellness in the Workplace' and ensuring that employee health comes to the forefront for the corporate clients she works with, who include Barclays, Karl Storz, Hilton, Hiscox Insurance, Porsche, Jaguar and Meta.

From self-publishing her first book, A Cupboard Full of Spices which covers both their medicinal and culinary uses with over 100 Indian recipes, to bringing her vision for The Garlic Story to life in these pages, Kumud is on a mission to educate and share her knowledge of food and wellbeing with others, creating positive outcomes and a lifetime of wellness for all.